An Outline of the Neolithic Culture of the Khasi-Jaintia Hills of Meghalaya, India

SOUTH ASIAN ARCHAEOLOGY SERIES

EDITED BY ALOK K. KANUNGO   No. 11

An Outline of the Neolithic Culture of the Khasi-Jaintia Hills of Meghalaya, India

An Archaeological Investigation

Marco Mitri

BAR International Series 2013
2009

Published in 2016 by
BAR Publishing, Oxford

BAR International Series 2013

An Outline of the Neolithic Culture of the Khasi-Jaintia Hills of Meghalaya, India

ISBN 9781407304632 paperback

ISBN 9781407335391 e-format

DOI https://doi.org/10.30861/9781407304632

A catalogue record for this book is available from the British Library

BAR Publishing is the trading name of British Archaeological Reports (Oxford) Ltd.
British Archaeological Reports was first incorporated in 1974 to publish the BAR
Series, International and British. In 1992 Hadrian Books Ltd became part of the BAR
group. This volume was originally published by John and Erica Hedges Ltd. in
conjunction with British Archaeological Reports (Oxford) Ltd / Hadrian Books Ltd,
the Series principal publisher, in 2009. This present volume is published by BAR
Publishing, 2016.

BAR
PUBLISHING

BAR titles are available from:

BAR Publishing
122 Banbury Rd, Oxford, OX2 7BP, UK
EMAIL   info@barpublishing.com
PHONE   +44 (0)1865 310431
FAX   +44 (0)1865 316916
www.barpublishing.com

Foreword

Alok Kumar Kanungo
Series Editor, South Asian Archaeology Series
International Series of British Reports

The International Series of British Archaeological Reports, with its c2000 titles to the present time, is undoubtedly one of the most important places of publication in the discipline of Archaeology. But it is a pity that works on the archaeology of South Asia have been less represented in the series than their interest and value deserves.

The archaeological record of South Asia (comprising India, Pakistan, Nepal, Bhutan, Bangladesh, Sri Lanka and the Maldives) is extremely rich. This wealth begins in the Lower Palaeolithic period and includes, for example, the Harappan Civilization, one of the oldest in the world (covering a very large area and having many unique features -- the most ancient known town planning, its architecture and high standards of civic hygiene, its art, iconography, paleography, numismatics and international trade). South Asia also has a large number of earlier, contemporary, and later Neolithic and Chalcolithic cultures. Moreover, what makes South Asia particularly significant for the study of past human behaviour is the survival of many traditional modes of life, like hunting-gathering, pastoralism, shifting cultivation, fishing, and fowling, the study of which throws valuable light on the reconstruction of past cultures. In the region there are a large number of government and semi-government institutions devoted to archaeological teaching and/or research in archaeology and a large and professionally trained body of researchers.

Of course, a number of universities and other institutions, in the area do have their own publication programmes and there are also reputed private publishing houses. However, British Archaeological Reports, a series of 30 years standing, has an international reputation and distribution system. In order to take advantage of the latter – to bring archaeological researches in South Asia to the notice of scholars in the western academic world – the South Asian Archaeology Series has been instituted within the International Series of British Archaeological Reports. This series (which it is hoped to associate with an institution of organization in the area) aims at publishing original research works of international interest in all branches of archaeology of South Asia.

Those wishing to submit books for inclusion in the South Asian Archaeology Series should contact the South Asian Archaeology Series Editor, who will mediate with BAR Publishing in Oxford. The subject has to be appropriate and of the correct academic standard (*curriculum vitae* are requested and books may be referred); instructions for formatting will be given, as necessary.

Dr. Alok Kumar Kanungo
Department of Archaeology
Deccan College Post-Graduate & Research Institute
Pune 411006
INDIA
email: alok_kanungo@yahoo.com

Preface

Reports of Neolithic findings from the Khasi and Jaintia hills of the central Meghalaya plateau, goes back to the year 1875 when Major Godwin-Austen reported about the finding of three celts from Shillong in the *Proceedings of the Asiatic Society of Bengal* (1875) and J. Cockburn's notes on stone implements from the Khasi hills reported in the same Journal (1879). These tools appear in the *Catalogue of Prehistoric Antiquities in Indian Museum,* by Coggin Brown (Calcutta, 1917) and A.H. Dani in his Ph.D. thesis which was published under the title *Pre and Proto-History of Eastern India,* (Calcutta, 1960). Thus, the Khasi hills found its place in the Pre-historic map of the country.

Field investigation however, did not take place until 1979, when a team of investigators from the Anthropology Department of Gawahati University located a Neolithic site close to the heart land of the Khasi hills at Umiam-Barapani. Explorations of the site continue till 1995 and a total number of 84 stone implements were collected during these explorations through surface collections. This site is designated as a Factory site by Archeologists. These initial findings provided a breakthrough which opened up scope for more intense field investigation concerning Neolithic period.

Working under the existing reports, this investigation attempted to understand the spread and extent of Neolithic culture in the Khasi and Jaintia hills with an aim to hypothetically establish its distribution pattern. The objective of this book is to basically work-out the relationship between the Neolithic cultures of the surrounding areas such as the reported sites of Daojali Hading of North Cachar Hills District of Assam and the sites of Sarataru and Marakdola of Karbi Anglong District of Assam with the Neolithic sites of the Khasi and Jaintia hills. This work also aimed at getting some insights into the migration patterns of the Neolithic people both from outside and within the area under-study.

It is imperative to understand the ethnographic population of these hills, if we are achieved more meaning out of the archaeological records since some features of the Neolithic experiences is still seen largely intact with the rural people of this region. Keeping this view in mind, this present work made an effort to provide as much ethnographic input as possible about the people, their history and culture. By applying the *Direct Historical Analogy* model, the Etnhoarchaeological data from these hills have greatly help to substantiate the archaeological findings. Thus much of the achievements made through this investigation are primarily due to the inputs generated out of the ethnographic information, mostly preserved in the oral form.

Although the Neolithic artefacts documented in this research were all collected from surface of the sites, they have however proved very crucial from an archaeological perspective, as these findings, have helped to provide the much needed breakthrough in Neolithic investigation of the area for a detail archaeological investigation in the future.

The building of hypotheses on intra-hills migration pattern during the Neolithic, linking the Neolithic phase with the Megalithic and Iron using phase and the hypothesis ascribing the continuity of occupation of these hills by the authors of the Neolithic tools to the period of the emergence of chiefdom societies and beginning of state formation is one the achievements of this project. Although there are some areas which requires sustentative evidences, this preliminary investigation has helped to open new dimension about the lesser-known prehistoric phase of the hills especially with regard to the Neolithic period.

Marco Mitri

II

Acknowledgements

I owe my gratitude to many people who have contributed greatly to the achievement of work.

As this work is based mainly on my doctoral thesis awarded by the North Eastern Hill University (NEHU), Shillong, India I am thankful to Dr. Cecile Mawlong, of the History department of NEHU my Ph.D. Supervisor, Prof. M. Momin HOD of History Department of NEHU, Shillong, Prof. David Syiemlieh, former HOD of History Department all the Teaching and Non-Teaching staff of History Department NEHU, Shillong.

I extend my gratitude to Dr. Tia Toshi Jamir of Nagaland University, Dr. David Titso of Deccan College, Pune, Mr. Danny Burke of National University, Ireland and Mr. Shngian Buhroi for helping me out with the reading materials.

There are those whom I shall ever remain grateful for helping me during the entire course of my field work and they are, Mr. Daniel Marwein an ex-student of UCC who provided me the first breakthrough during my initial field work Late Mr. G. Sumer, Archeologist, State Culture Department Government of Meghalaya, Mr. Teron, the Head Man of Liarbang village (2005), Mr. Madur and his friends from Mawbri Village, Late Mr. Syiem of Mawbri village, Mr Primus from Umswai Village, Mr. Lebes from Mawlyndep village, Mr. Finly Rogers Syiem of Umroi village, Mr. Bahduh Kharumnuid of Law Nongthroh village, Mr. Mr. Rymphang Nongsiej of Sutnga Village, Mr. Phelas and Mr. Kodri Syiemlieh of Nongspung village, Mr. Gatphoh of Govt' Quarters San-Mer, the Thawmuid family of Myrkhan village, Mr. Poletson of Nongkhrah village, Mr. Dipshon Nongbri of Lumsohpet Bneng Committee and Mr. Trueman Shylla for the materials from Jaintia hills.

I should also thank all my friends and colleagues who have extended their helping hand in their fields of specialization during the course of my Ph.D. project. I should mention them by their names; Mr. Karmelstar Makdoh for the drawings, Mr. Lalnunkima for the maps, Mr. Moning Monsang for the proof reading, Mr. Mansan Lyngdoh, Geologist DMR, Shillong for the identification of the stone materials, Mr. Alpha Sawkmie, Mr. Richard Wahlang, and Ms. Barbie Lyngdoh, for accompanying me during my field work, Dr. Ashish Malhotra and Mr. Rudolf Manih for the Spectra Analysis of some of the materials, Mr. Jim Marak, my colleagues from UCC and Mr. Ovidio Kurbah, and Mr. David Diamai my friends from Mawlai, and my little niece Joanna for being so helpful to me during the writing part .

I should extent my special thanks to Dr. Alok Kanungo for accepting this research book for publication in this Series.

Last but not the least, I Thank the Almighty for all the Unseen Blessings.

I dedicate this work to my Beloved Parents.

Marco Mitri

Contents

List of Figures

List of Plates

x

CHAPTER 1

THE KHASI AND JAINTIA HILLS OF MEGHALAYA
An Introduction

Area of Research

This investigation covers the central and eastern parts of the state of Meghalaya (Figure 1). The state was carved out from the erstwhile state of Assam and made a full-fledged state on 21st January 1971 (under the North-Eastern Re-organisation Areas Act of 1971). The state shares 423 km of its border with Bangladesh in the south and the Brahmaputra valley stretches across the entire northern border. It is located between 25⁰2' N to 26⁰6' N Latitudes and 89⁰48' E to 92⁰50' E Longitudes with a total area of 22,429 sq. km (Sharma, 2003, p.5)

The Meghalaya plateau consists of the Khasi, Jaintia and Garo hills along the outliner formed by the Assam ranges. The plateau is the detached north-eastern extension of the Peninsular India; part of it lies buried under the alluvium deposited by the Ganga-Brahmaputra river systems which is commonly term as the Malda gap. The Khasi and Jaintia hills, which forms the central and eastern part of the Meghalaya plateau is the main focus of this research. The Khasi and Jaintia hills are located between 25⁰1' and 26⁰5' North Latitude and between 90⁰47' to 92⁰52' East Longitude (The Khasi hills is located between 25⁰10' to 25⁰ 25' North Latitude and 91⁰ 0' to 90⁰ 30' East Longitude and the Jaintia hills lies between 20⁰ 58' to 26⁰ 3' North Latitude and 91⁰ 59' to 92⁰ 51').

The administration of the Khasi hills is divided into three districts viz. the East Khasi hills district, West Khasi hills district and the Ri-Bhoi district in the north. The Jaintia hills which forms the eastern part of the state of Meghalaya

is a composite district of its own. Politically, the two hills are bounded on the north by the Kamrup district of Assam, on the south by the Sylhet district of Bangladesh, on the west by the Garo hills districts of Meghalaya and on the east by the Karbi Anglong district of Assam. The total extent of the area covered by the Khasi and Jaintia hills is 14,375 Sq. km (*Ibid*, p.19).

Physiography

The Khasi and the Jaintia hills represent the remnants of an ancient plateau of the Pre-Cambrian Indian peninsular shield and they reach a height of 600-1800 m above the mean sea level. Therefore these hills are considered to be a true plateau. Physiographically, these hills can be divided into three distinct sub-units (Figure2) (*Ibid*, pp. 18-21):

1) The Northern undulating hills;

2) The Central Upland zone; and

3) The Southern precipitous zone.

The northern part of the Khasi hills is marked by gentle slopes of undulating hills that gradually merged with the Brahamaputra valley through the sub-montane region known as the *Ri-Bhoi* area. There are three terraces of peneplain which can be identified throughout this region and they are formed at 150 m, 300 m and 600 m (contour) level respectively. This region has an overall average elevation of 170-820 m above sea level and descends towards the north.

1

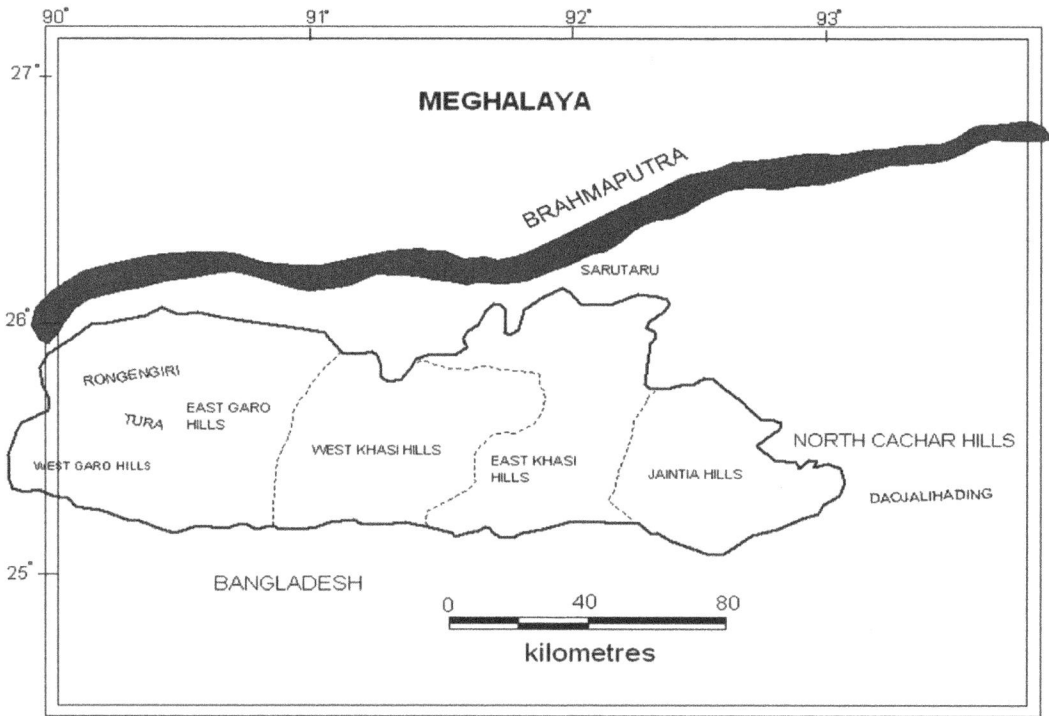

Figure 1: Area of Research

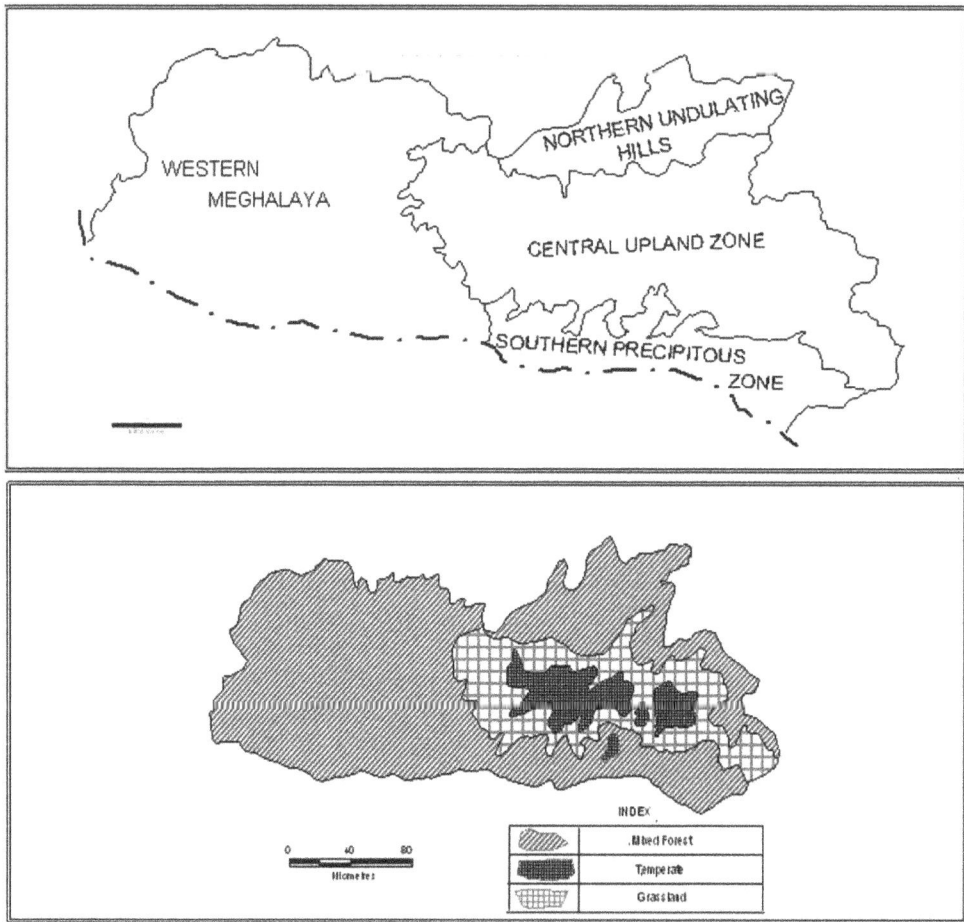

Figure 2: Physiographic Units and Vegetation Type

The central upland zone running from east to west is the dominant physiographic unit of the plateau. It covers more than one third of central and eastern Meghalaya. A 1500 m contour, forms the outer boundary and largely consists of rolling uplands dissected by river valleys. This zone also has the remnants of many peneplain surfaces ranging from 1500 to 2083 m above sea level.

The southern section of the plateau includes the steepest slopes of the state and is locally known as the *War* country. It stands as an escarpment and it has been subjected to the fluvial erosion caused by extremely heavy rainfall resulting in the formation of a number of platforms. Three sub-sections or platforms like structures have been identified and they are known as Cherrapunji, Langkyrdem and Mawsynram platform. A number of caves containing stalactites and stalagmites are also found in this zone.

The Jaintia hills have more flat lands than the Khasi hills. It forms a contiguous part of central plateau with the same physiographic divisions and extends up to the Kopli River. This marks the eastern boundary of the Jaintia hills. This region slopes from west to east, from 1450 to 1000 m above sea level and acts as a watershed between the Surma and the Bhramaputra valley.

Climatic Condition

Unlike other parts of India, the climatic condition of the Meghalaya Plateau is largely controlled by elevation and physical relief. The pressure cells located in Northwest India and the depression of the Bay of Bengal and the South significantly influence the climatic fluctuation in the state. The Khasi and Jaintia hills experience a moderate climate. The foothills region of the south and sub-montane region of the north and central, have prevailing warm and humid climate in summer and pleasantly warm climate in winter. On an average, the two places experience a temperature of 24^0C throughout most of the summer i.e. March-November, and about 15^0 in winters i.e. between December and February. In winter the average temperature in the upland zone during the night falls to $4-5^0$C.

The southern part of the plateau receives the heaviest rainfall with an annual average of 12670 mm. On the whole, the Khasi and Jaintia hills receive an average annual rainfall of 7700 mm with more than three-fourth of the rainfall falling during the monsoon seasons.

The present climate pattern of the Khasi and Jaintia hills in a year is shown below (Simon, 1991, p.27):

January:	Heavy morning dew and hoar frost, but generally rainless
February:	Heavy morning dew and hoar frost but short spell of rain during the middle of the month
March–April:	Generally dry, and winds continue for several weeks. Early rain starts at the end of April.
May:	Warm and dry, and rains become more frequent.
June-August:	Period of heavy rainfall
September:	Rain continues but starts to fall in frequency
October:	Rainy days stop
November:	Cold season sets in. Frosts in high altitudes around the end of the month
December:	Cold seasons advances. Frost becomes more widespread

Flora and Fauna

The Khasi and Jaintia hills are largely dissected and covered by dense forest over wide areas. The tropical type of broad leaf vegetation covers the area having an elevation of 990 M above sea level. The warm temperate conifer vegetation occurs in the area which has an elevation of 1300 M above sea level. In several suitable areas, there is a mixture of temperate, tropical and sub-tropical vegetation (Figure 2). The Sacred grooves at the central upland in Shillong Peak, Mawphlang and Mawsmai represent the type of original forest vegetation that must have covered these hills in prehistoric times (*Ibid*). These pockets contain a great diversity of flora species. The secondary forest of the **Pinus kesiya** or the pine forests are very common in the places which has an elevation higher than 900 m above sea level.

The faunal composition of the Khasi and Jaintia hills region is closely connected with the geomorphological evolution of the area. The region served as a faunal gateway through which the Indo-Chinese elements of oriental fauna and paleoartic montane fauna spread to the main sub continent (*Ibid*, p.23). The tropical and sub-tropical moist evergreen-forest ensures the survival of rich mammalian fauna and also other groups of animal life. The gibbon (*Hoolock*), different variety of wild cat (*Felis*), the Himalayan black bear (Selenarctos *thibenthanus*), barking deer (Muntiacus *muntjak*) etc are some of the common wild fauna of the region. Birds can be seen in abundance in these forests especially in places with lower altitudes. The red vented bulbul (Picnonotus *cafer bengalesis*), the thick billed green pigeon (Teron *curverostra nepalensis)*, number of myna species, the red jungle fowl (Gallus *gallus*) etc. are some of the commonly found birds in the region. Besides mammals, birds and reptiles, the hills are also homes to a number of interesting amphibian species and their groups, many of which have adapted to the hill streams.

An Outline about the People

The Khasi and Jaintia hills which is covered under the present investigation derived their names from the word 'Khasi' (which includes the 'Pnar or Jaintia') tribe who are the inhabitants of the area. The earliest reference to the name can be found in Renell's map published in 1780 in which the name appeared as 'Cussey' (Chowdhury, 1996, p.5). Various writers have spelt the word 'Khasi' in different ways, such as Cossyah, Khassyah, Kasia, etc. The present name was adopted for the first time by the Christian Missionaries at Cherrapunjee

for use in their printed works. The origin of the word is still shrouded in mystery and till date no satisfactory explanation has been made. Based on the report of David Scott, Pemberton stated that the people called themselves *Khyee* (Pemberton, 1835, p.219). Dalton, referred to the people by the name *Khasia*, a term often used by the people from the plains (Dalton, 1872, p.54). Godwin Austin felt that the word might have been derived from the Aryan word *Ghasi*, meaning grassy in reference to the condition of the upper landscape which is a contrast to the forest-clad valleys of the slopes and the outer hills. He said that the people never pronounced the hard 'g', and in all the Aryan originated words, the letter 'g' is pronounced as 'k' (Godwen-Austin, 1872, pp. 122-143). Local traditions on the other hand, suggest that the name 'Khasi' was derived from the name of a woman called *Si*, and it was prefixed by the feminine connotation '*Ka*'. Therefore the actual word should be spelt as '*Kasi*', which is an eponymous ancestress of the Khasi people (Namita Cathrine Shadap Sen, 1981, p.1). The confusion over the root of the word will however continue to be debated and a more philological research is necessary to arrive at a plausible explanation of the term.

Regarding the original home of the people, not a single authentic source of historical evidence has been found till date. Most of the inferences that have been put forward with respect to the original homeland of the people were derived mainly from traditions and linguistic affinity of the Khasi people with those who inhabited some parts of the south-east Asian countries. Based on the above sources, it has been said that the Khasis came to their present habitat from the eastern direction. They came from Assam through the Patkoi hills and this same route has been used by other immigrants from Burma such as the Ahoms of Assam (Gurdon, 1914, pp. 11-12). The migration route of the people is further confounded by the retention of the names of certain places such as the name *Makachang* which the Khasis use to refer to the Himalayas. This evidence is used by some scholars to speculate that the people might have once settled around the Himalayas (Bareh, 1967, p.12). This is quite apparent in the oral traditions of certain prominent clans of the west Khasi hills who have always pointed towards the east as their migration route (*ibid*, p.15). Without any doubt, this strong tendency of westward movement among the people can be taken as another ground of support to the existing speculation that the east was the original homeland of the Khasis.

Settlement, Race and Language

The Khasi tribe is a common nomenclature applied to the inhabitants of the central and eastern Meghalaya Plateau. The Khasi tribe is divided into various sub-groups which has been identified mainly on the basis of their settlement patterns; the *Khyr-iem* (or the Khasis) who occupy the upland zone of central track of the Meghalaya plateau, the *War-Khasi* occupy the southern precipitous terrain of the Khasi hills, the *War-Jaintia* groups who occupy the low elevated lying belt of Jaintia hills, the *Bhoi* groups that occupy the entire northern slopes of the central Meghalaya Plateau and the *Synteng* or the *Pnar* groups that occupy the eastern uplands of Meghalaya plateau also known as Jaintia hills (Figure 1). How long ago has the settlement pattern assumed its present shape, is a question, yet to be answered. On the of basis conjectures supported by folk tradition, the segregation can be best linked with the different waves of migration of the Khasis into their present habitat (Bareh, 1991, p.24). As far as the population is oncerned, one of the earliest record made in 1870 showed that the Khasi-Jaintia hills had an estimated population of approximately 1,18,925 people (Hunter, 1879, p.215).

On the basis of the general physical characteristics, the Khasi have been racially classified as Mongoloid. Although typical Mongoloid features are quite noticeable among the Khasis, it is scientifically not plausible to outrightly classify the people without placing them within the broad anthropological parameters. On the basis of various anthropometric survey conducted on the peole from time, a broad categrisation place the Khasis as differ from the *Brachycephalic* (broad-headed) true mongoloid feature, and they fall under the *Mesophalic* head-form (short-headed) (Raychodhury, 1935, p.1).

Although in general, the Khasis possess short stature and mesophalic head shape, there are variations in the face and nose. While some anthropologists' measurement showed more evidence of *mesorrhine* (medium) form of nose, others reveal high occurrence of *platyrrhine* (broad) nose form. There is also a disagreement among scholars with respect to the facial index. In trying to establish their racial and ethnic affinity, the Khasis have been subjected to more anthropometric studies than any other tribe. Even then, no unanimity has been arrived at with regard to the physical characteristics of the different groups within the Khasi tribe itself, not to talk about a comparative study with the other neighbouring tribes having allied mongoloid features. Efforts have also been made to establish a relationship on the basis of the blood-group pattern. The Khasis' blood-group pattern showed high percentage concentration of blood-group B and AB which link them with Tibet and China (Shadap, 1981, p.16). This blood-group evidence somehow goes in contrast with the existing notion that the Khasis have more racial affinity with south-east Asia than to China or Tibet (Chowdhury, 1996, p.32). The absence of unanimity among scholars with regard to the physical features of the Khasis has been attributed largely to the great admixture of racial traits which took place in the adjoining and contiguous areas of south and east Asiatic region.

In their present habitat, the Khasis are surrounded on all directions by other groups speaking the Tibeto-Burman and Indo-Aryan languages. J.R. Logan (*Ibid*, p.34) is perhaps one of the earliest writers who demonstrated the relationship between the Khasis and certain people of further India along with the Mons, Palung and Khmer of South East Asia on the basis of vocabularies. Linguistics studies indicate that the Khasis form a group of the Mon-Khmer language that belongs to the Austro-Asiatic type which is one branch of the 'Austric' family of languages, a theory developed by Father W. Schmidt. (Gurdon, 1914, p.xix). Besides the Khasis, the Austro-

Asiatic group of languages also include the Munda language, chief of which are the Mundari, Santali, Nicobares, Munda, Santal, Ho and Gadaba of Chotanagpur plateau, the Mon of South Burma and South-west Thailand, Khmer of Combodia, Wa and Palung of Burma, Sakai and Semang tribal of Malaya and many other insignificant tribes. In the form of speech, however there is a great difference between the Mon-Khmer and the Mundari with respect to the grammar, vocabulary, phonetics and syntax. The most distinct feature is that, the Mon-Khmer which includes the Khasi, forms, the monosyllabic groups, whereas the Mundari which includes the Nicobarese, make use of polysyllables (Bareh, 1967, p.17). Although, polysyllabic words are numerous in the Khasi language, they are generally seen as compounds with recognizable monosyllabic root words (Shadap, 1981, p.52). The present-day geographical distribution of the Mon Khmer languages seems to indicate that the language originated from northern Thailand and there are as many as 80 Mon-Khmer linguistic groups that exist around the world (Bareh, 1967, p.17). The Mon-Khmer family of languages probably originated in the region of northern Thailand, and the jungles of this region being the home of the Mrabri or *Phi Tong Luang* who are considered as one of the most primitive people in the world, and who speak the Mon-Khmer language (Shadap, 1981, p. 54)

Glottochrolnologists, have developed a hypothesis that the deviation of one language from another proceeds at a uniform rate and on the basis of this hypothesis, Professor Eugénie Henderson of London University concludes that the Khasi, Mon, Khmer and Viatnamese had a common language until about 2400 B.C. Prof. H.L. Shroto of the same University, on the other hand, points to a much remoter period and concludes that Khasi language appeared at about 4300 B.C. (*Ibid*, p.56). On the basis of the linguistic affinity, some scholars (Chowdhury, 1996, p.37.), associate the Austric-speaking population with the advent of the proto-Austroloid racial element who entered India only after the Negroid element.

The genetic evidences on the basis of Y-chromosome SNP and STR data analysis from 1222 individuals of 25 Indian populations may provide additional evidence while dealing with the migration of the Khasi population. From the studies, it has been found that haplogroup O-M95 is found all over Southeast Asia, while in India it is restricted to the regions where Austro-Asiatic populations are concentrated. It has also been observed that, haplogroup O-M95 is found in a relatively high frequency among the Khasi (41%) as also with other Austro Asiatic populations of India (highest among the Mundari 55%). This may underscore that the Mundari, Khasi and Mon-Khmer groups of India are not only linguistically related but also genetically linked. This haplogroup has been reported to be absent or present in low frequency in other linguistic groups of India, suggesting a distinct genetic identity of the Indian Austro-Asiatic populations. The Khasis on the other hand also show relatively high frequency of haplogroup O-M122 (29%) and given that populations of the Khasi sub-family are concentrated in the regions North of Burma and Thailand, it is possible that Khasi populations may have migrated from Southeast Asia to India. However, the presence of O-M122 in the Khasi is observed to be due to gene flow from the neighboring Garo population (having 55% of O-M122), further suggesting that the Khasi population was initially devoid of this haplogroup. Thus it has been postulated that the Mundari and Khasi populations had separated long back and the latter have probably gone to Southeast Asia, via the northeast Indian corridor, as reflected in their geographic distribution. Therefore, the Mundari populations appear to be one of the earliest sources of populations from which the Khasi and Mon-Khmer populations have separated quite early and migrated to and settled in Southeast Asia (Vikrant Kumar *et. al.*, 2008).

The Society

A notable feature of the Khasi society is their 'matrilineal system'. Regarding the antiquity of the system, there is one reference which appeared in the Calcutta Review of volume xiv May 1867 about the ancient Assam which offers some historical validation. The reference states that, after Heun Tsang's visit to Assam, the king of Kashmir who ruled between 714 and 750 A.D. attempted a vain invasion on the Jaintia kingdom which was referred to as *"Stri-Rajya"* or kingdom with a female ruler (Lyngdoh, 1962, p.iii). In contrast to the other tribes around them, the Khasi matrilineal system when viewed from the region's perspective has come to acquire a unique character. And it can perhaps be treated as an institution which has been preserved since the prehistoric period. This unique institution along with its distinctive linguistic affinity provides a clear indicator to the isolated character of the people in the context of the region they inhabited. These two evidences indirectly point to a very different (pre) historical course which the Khasis have gone through. The matrilineal system may also be seen as mode of defense mechanism which allows the community to retain its distinct identity.

From the genetic evidence, the presence of genetic marker haplotype O-M122 on the Khasi population (the genetic marker being quite high among the Garos), does reflect some social implication. Inferring from the genetic sampling which was mentioned above, it probably shows that the Garo element is represented in the Khasi genetic makeup. The survey gives an implication that when there is a mix between a Khasi and a Garo, the progeny invariably claimed a Khasi identity. The *absorption capacity* of the Khasis may be best attested to the matrilineal system which appears to operate as a protective instrument, deliberately adopted to preserve their identity, a system which acted as a *safety valve* to counter the socio-political pressure from the surrounding Tibeto-Burman speaking patrilineal/patriarchal communities. This, then allow us to speculate that the matrilineal institution of the Khasis made a huge impact on its closest neighbours, the Garos, who probably adopted the system right from the earlier times. The process of adoption is ethnographically observed among some of the Mikir communities who lived along the borders of Khasi and Jaintia hills, some of whom never claimed to be Khasis, but adopted much of the Khasi culture, most glaring, being the

matrilineal system[1]. The recent observation made on the neighbouring Mikir community, can be hypothetically used as a model to demonstrate the transitional phase of Garo adoption of Khasi matriliny thereby allowing us to speculate that the Garos were among the first Tibeto-Burman speaking-population, who had interacted with the Khasis[2].

The social structure of the Khasis is composed of the *Kurs* or the clans and all of them trace their origin to one primeval mother called *Ka Iawbei Tynrai* who is the ancestress of the whole clan. In the clan line, the next is followed by *Ka Iawbei Tymmen* or the great grandmother who is the founder of the sub-clan, then finally comes the *Ka Iawbei Khynraw* or grandmother who is the ancestress of the family or the *Iing* (Gurdon, 1914, p.63). From the male line, *U Thawlang* is revered as the ancestral father of the clan and *U Suidnia* is the eldest maternal uncle of the clan and the of *Ka Iawbei Tynrai*. The Khasi marriage system is strictly exogamous, and it is considered a great taboo to marry within the clan or within the sister clans[3] who traces their origin to the same ancestress.

The origin of clans among the Khasis is attested to the different traditions to which each clan have managed to preserved in the clans' oral history for generations to generations. Some clans adopted their mother or father's name, and there are others which bear totemistic name and trace their origin to some species of animals, trees or plants such as *Shrieh* or monkey, *Tham* or crab, *Bee* or ngap, *Diengdoh* or wooden trough, *Pathaw* or pumkin, *Sohkhia* or cucumber, *Malngiang* or a type of fish etc. There is no record from recent ethnographic study to

---

[1] This study is based on a random ethnographic survey conducted during the exploration for archaeological sites along the Mikir-Ri-Bhoi borders around the villages of Iapngar, Tyrso and the adjoining villages. Some people from these villages claimed to be Khasis and adopted Khasi matrilineal system but bear non-Khasi clan title.

[2] It has to be noted that such a historical process of adoption by the Garos is not based on any substantial proof and is still at a level of conjecture only.

[3] Which may bear different name(s), but are probably branches of, once the same clan. This knowledge passes on from generation to generations in the clan.

prove, that clans with totemistic names maintain any taboo on eating or killing the plants and animals whose name they still retain as identity of the of the clan. But, traditional people believe that such a taboo prevailed in the past, like for example, the Malngiang clan considered pork a taboo, to the Ryntathiang clan eating, of one species of citrus fruit (*Soh Nairiang*) is considered a taboo, the Pathaw clan considered pumkin a taboo etc. Hence it cannot be said with certainty if totemistic practice prevailed or not among the Khasis. Some scholars, however, argue that the Khasi exogamy, arose from totemism, inferring that, the taboo from eating an animal (or plants) belonging to his totem likewise connote the danger of marrying someone within his own totem (Roy, 1936, p.384) There are also clans which bear the names of their ancient settlement, while others traced their descent from the goddess from whom the ruling clan originated (Gurdon, 1914, pp. 70-71). A clan having a common descent may not necessarily bear the same name, because in the process of time, many events may have taken place encouraging the clan to assume different names. But, there is a strong tradition which lives and is preserved in the minds of the people that guides each clan to trace its affiliation (if there is any) to one another through a common descent. Through this conventional method, a particular clan can trace its affiliated clans. These clans are nothing but an overgrown family, and they are formally knitted together through the institution of ancestor worship, vividly expressed in the mortuary practice. In the pre-Christian mortuary practice, the clan would gather together and relocate their post-cremated bones from their individual family cists to a common clan sepulcher.

The matrilineal system of the Khasis renders the position of the women more or less equal to that of men in social matters. The women being considered as the progenitors of the clan are regarded in high esteem. However, in political matters the women are not allowed to participate, as this is considered to be the exclusive domain of males. The social position of the women is well reflected in the inheritance of property in which the males have no share in the family's possession. In theory the ancestral property would always be given to the youngest female of the family who automatically enjoys the lion's share of the family possession, but in practice she remains only a custodian of that possession. She is not allowed to dispose off the family possession which she inherited without the consent of the family or clan members especially the maternal uncles. Owing to this reason perhaps, that ancestral house or the *Iing Seng* is held with sanctity. The house is a place for hosting generations of youngest daughters and offers refuge to other members of the family and the clan. At the same time, it is also the center for all religious ceremonies which involve the family. Owing to the said system, property falls under two categories; (i) Inalienable (ii) alienable. The first type is known as *Nongtymmen* or the ancestral property which cannot be disposed off without the consent of the entire family members. The second type is known as *Nongkhynraw* or self acquired property that which can be disposed at will.

The retention of the matrilineal system by the Khasis may have been closely linked with the idea of *land ownership*, and the role of a clan as the guardian of the land became more important especially after the Khasis came into contact with the surrounding Tibeto-Burman groups. Because of close proximity, inter-marriage with the latter became inevitable, which probably prompted the Khasis to adopt a *system* that is congenial for preserving their identity and at the same time provided them with a sense of security over the ownership of the territory which they have made their claim upon. The matrilineal institution thus, served as an instrument of peaceful cultural assimilation adopted by the Khasis because of the pressure impacted by the neighbouring patrilineal/patriarchal groups surrounding them. The presence of a large number of Khasi clans with the prefix *Khar*[4], certainly corroborate the *absorption capacity* of the Khasi tribe, thereby attesting to the peaceful cultural assimilation of the community with the neighbouring tribes.

---

[4] A short form of the word '*Dkhar*' which in the Khasi philology, denotes an 'outsider or foreigner' of the tribe.

Religion

To the Khasis, religion is literally understood as *Niam*, a term which was probably either loaned from the non-tribal word *Niom*, or may have originated itself from the word *Nia* which literally means 'word' in the Khasi dialect. While tracing the root of the word *Niam* from the word *Nia*, there is still so much space for debates and conjectures. In Khasi religion, the word *Nia* is always associated with another word *Jutang*, meaning a 'covenant'. Thus, even if the word *Niam* may have been loaned, that does not imply that the Khasi are without a concept of religion at all. Khasi religion is associated with the 'covenant' through a 'word' that they made with God, who is identified as *U Blei Nongthaw or* the God of creation. This covenant is preserved in the Khasi folk lore of '*U Sohpet Bneng*'[5]. Some scholar are of the opinion that there is a notion of the feminine attribute in the Godhead with whom is entrusted the care and control of the universe (Roy, 1936, p.384) and she is known as *Ka Blei Synshar* or the ruling Goddess (Gurdon, 1914, p.105). There are others who argued that the supreme God, is also revered to, as the great ancestress and hence, the term *Ka Blei Nongshynshar*. The suffix *Ka* which denoted femininity became prominent in the Khasi religion due to the influence of the matrilineal institution. There are minor gods who are the anthropomorphic beings (Shadap, 1981, p.209). These anthropomorphized deities are of terrestrial, celestial and cosmic order, such as the tender hearted goddess, the Sun or Ka *Sngi*, the moon or *U Bnai*, the Toad or *ka Hynroh*, the god of the hills, *U kyllang, U Symper*, god of thunder or *U Pyrthat*, the stream goddess or *ka Iam, ka Ngot*. There are presiding deities like the deity presiding over water or *Lei Umtong*, the village deity or *U Ryngkew U Basa, U Phan U Kyrpad*, deities of diseases *Ka Rih, Ka Khlam, Ka Tyrut*. The above mentioned are few of the innumerable classification of Khasi manifestations of God. The Khasis offer sacrifices and performed egg-breaking ceremonies to propitiate the gods and goddesses. All these divinities were agents of the supreme God. In practice, the traditional Khasi religion is animistic in content and propagates spirit-worship, both good and evil spirits. The other principal feature of the Khasi religion is the 'ancestor worship'. In such ceremonies, the priest or the *Lyngdohs*, who are well versed in the art of necromancy, played a very important role in propitiation of the spirits.

The Megalithic Culture

Von Furer Haimendorf stated that *"There exist no race in the Asiatic mainland which had developed Megalithic technique to such a degree as the Khasis, their row of huge menhirs, bone repository built on gigantic slab...are among the most impressive Megalithic monuments"*(Haimendorf, 1943, p.173). The Megalithic tradition in the Khasi and Jaintia Hills was a living tradition till very recent times. The megalithic monuments are widely distributed throughout the length and breadth of the Khasi and Jaintia hills. A good number of reports have been published on the Megalithic tradition of the Khasi and Jaintia hills beginning with the records of the colonial workers in the 19th century. These records have served as an important source of information about the cultural practice at the time when the tradition was still vibrant, especially concerning description about the monuments and their functional significance. However, it is rather unfortunate that till today not a single chronological date can be assigned to this practice, although one scholar is of the opinion that, probably the bone repositories such as the cairns and the cists pre-dates the thirteen century A.D. (Mawlong, 2004, p.37). It is also not certain whether the practice of erecting stones among the Khasis was intrusive into their culture or had evolved from within.

A classification of the Megalithic monuments of the Khasi and Jaintia Hills was comprehensively dealt with in the Ph.D. Thesis of Cecile Mawlong, which is briefly discussed below (Mawlong, 1996, pp. 27-60).

---

[5] A detail description of the folk tale is mention in the later chapter. In this research, the folk tale is examined with an aim to contextualized the archeological evidences.

On the basis of morphology, the megalithic remains in the Khasi and Jaintia are grouped into five broad groups:

Group A: Menhirs, Alignments and Avenues.

Group B: Dolmens.

Group C: Cists, Cairns and Cairn-Cists.

Group D: Stone Circles.

Group E: Stone Cremation Platforms.

On functionally grounds, the megalithic monuments mentioned may be classified into two distinct groups:

(A) Funerary Stones or *Mawbynna Niam* further classify into:
1. *Mawkjat/Mawlynti/ Mawksing,* *[6] stones of the foot or leg/ stones of the way or path/stones of the drum.
2. *Mawumkoi and Mawtyrut,* * stones of the Purificatory Tank and stones of the Female evil spirit.
3. *Mawklim,* * stones of adultery.
4. *Kpep,* * the Platform of cremation.
5. *Jaka Syang Syieng,* * place of drying and purifying the bones before they are interned into the clan cist.
6. *Mawsyieng,* * bone repositories which are structurally indentified with the cists and cairns.

(B) Memorial Stones or *Mawbynna Nam*
1. *Mawkni-Mawiawbei and Mawpud-Mawpyrsa,* * stones of the maternal uncles-female ancestress, and stones for demarcating boundaries-stones of maternal nephew.
2. *Mawthawlang, Mawkiaw-kha, and Maw Khun-Kha* * stones of the progenitor of the clan, stones of the paternal ancestress and stones of descendants of the male relatives.
3. *Mawkni Syiem, Mawiawbei, and MawPyrsa Syiem* * stones in honour of the dead chief, stones of the ancestress

of the chief and stones of the maternal nephew of the chiefs.
4. *Mawbynna,* * memorial stones erected for important events such as political, economic and social nature.
5. *Mawbri, Mawsam* * stones that demarcate private lands (either of individual, family or clan), and stones which are erected at the junction of the above two lands.

The cairns are therefore considered as the most ancient form of Megalithic practice, and they are found mostly in the northern part of the plateau. They are a heap of stones which are functionally treated as synonymous with the cists (Shadap, 1981, p.208). It has been opined that the megalithic tradition in these hills are closely linked to the concepts of unity of the maternal ancestry and social continuity, as a greater percentage of such memorials are dedicated to the ancestors of the matrilineal kin group (Mawlong, 2004, p.36). The monuments are also linked with concepts of fertility and social merit and a process involving the struggles among members of the society, over exercise of social power as such structures legitimised the rank and status of the dominant groups in society over others (*Ibid*, p.49).

A Brief Political History of the Khasi and Jaintia Hills

At the time of the advent of the British into the hills during the 19th Century, the Khasi hills were divided into 26 independent chieftainships. These chieftainships combined in a loose confederacy, but this did not materially affect their isolated independent existence. The Khasi and Jaintia hills were made into a new district in 1835 after the British took over the control of the region.

It has also been noted that the earliest reference of the word 'Khasi' occur in the paraphrase work of Sankaradeva's, *Bhagavata Purana* (Shadap, 1981, p.5). Several records of the Khasis can be found in the Ahom *Buranjis* or the court chronicles of the Ahom kings of Assam as these provide the earliest historical reference to the people living in the hills. However, since the

---

[6] * Literally translated.

Ahoms had more interaction with the kings of the Jaintia hills, these records give more reference about Jaintia hills and only stray accounts are made about the Khasi hills. Among them, the *Jayantia Buranji* provides information on the relations of the Ahom kings with the Hindu kingdom of Jaintiapur ruled by the Jiantia kings. Other *Buranjis* also contains references about the people of the hills and such accounts are mostly in relation with the Jaintia kings.

Actual historical records of the Khasi people started only with the coming of the Europeans. The first contact between the Khasis and the Europeans can be traced back to the Diwani of Bengal-1765, when the neighboring district of Sylhet became part of the area under the Diwani. The Europeans were actually brought into contact with the people because of their interest on the lime quarries available on the hills (Hunter, 1879, p.205). The first European to write on the Khasis was Robert Lindsay, a collector of the East India Company of Sylhet, who brought interesting accounts about the people and refer to them as a "a tribe of independent Tartars" that had direct relation with China (Gurdon, 1914, p.xv). Then, the work of R.B.Pemberton provided us with reference about the attack launched by Major Hinneker in 1774 in retaliation to the aggressive policy of the Jaintia king in Sylhet (Pemberton, 1835, p.23) The most detailed and lengthy description of the Khasi people is found in the work of P.R.T. Gurdon, "The Khasis". Though the book is more of an ethnographical than historical work, it is a very useful record about the people. Gurdon provided a comprehensive account about the economic life of the people during that time, the prevailing social system, the tribal religious beliefs and institutions and the nature of state organization of the people. As a deputy commissioner of the district where the Khasis inhabited, he had a long and close acquaintance with the people and their language. His monograph thus offers the closest glimpse of the people, their society and culture during the period when modern ideas had not made a deep impression in the minds of the Khasis. The work of P.C. Choudhuri (Choudhuri, 1966, p.81) contains some sections

which refer to the Khasis and Jaintias. Sir Edward Gait's "History of Assam" (1963) also made a reference about the political history of the Jaintias and the Khasis. Stray references about the Khasi people and their culture can be found in the works of ethnographers mostly in form of articles that are widely scattered in various journals of humanities[7]. These materials provided some of the oldest references about the people of the region and their culture.

In recent years, there has been a steady increase in the number of publications on subjects dealing with the culture of the people in the region. Local scholars[8], have added more on the existing materials, and such works have greatly contributed to the growth of literature on culture and early history of the people in the region. Side by side, there are also other works written in the vernacular dialect (language), and these works have come up as very useful source of information especially on the untouched areas in the field of culture and history[9].

The Present Work

Although quite a fair amount of literature dealing with the history and culture have been published, a vast area of open space still remain untouched, especially in the field of pre-history. This research is an effort to expose the distribution of prehistoric Neolithic sites in the region under study which encompasses the entire part of the central Meghalaya plateau. Except for the discovery of some stone artifacts from a single site of Umiam-Barapani, nothing much has been written about the Neolithic culture of the Khasi-Jaintia hills. Thus, the pre-historic situation in these hills is still largely unknown. The present research is the first ever attempt in this line to expand the knowledge about the region beyond the period of oral and written history. Through the science of archaeology and the application of its various

---

[7] *Journal of the Asiatic Society of Bengal, Man, Man In India, The Antropological Journal of Great Britain and Ireland,* etc.
[8] Hamlet Bareh, Namita Catherine Shadap Sen, J.N. Choudhry, Pristilla Lyngdoh (See Bibliography)
[9] Homiwell Lyngdoh, Philomena Kharakor, G. Costa, (See Bibliography)

approaches, this investigation is an effort to establish the distribution and spatial extent of Neolithic culture in these hills and to come up with some form of hypothesis regarding the continuity and change in settlement in the settlement pattern of the Khasi and Jaintia hills going back to the Neolithic level. This research which is a preliminary effort to expose the Stone Age scenario of the hills may leave behind some questions which will open the flood gates for more pre-historic research in the region.

CHAPTER 2

THE NEOLITHIC

Meaning and Concepts

The conventional term 'Neolithic' is defined in archaeological literature as a 'cultural label' (Narasimhaiah, 1990, Foreword). The Neolithic period marked a significant shift in the mode of human-cultural developments which, to a large extent, distinguished itself from the other developments that took place throughout the entire Stone Age period preceding it. The period can also be synonymously defined in terms of the evolution of an entirely new mode of human survival-strategy resulting in the birth of a new concept in prehistoric studies known as the 'Neolithic culture'. The term 'Neolithic', is an evolutionary scheme, a form of economy, a set of social relations and on the whole a cultural phenomenon (Thomas,1991, p.13). The Neolithic cultural phase had come to occupy a very significant place in history of human cultural evolution for two basic reasons; firstly, it stood as a watershed between the stone-age culture and the age of metal, and secondly, it has been used as the decisive measuring index which consciously or unconsciously enabled us to measure the rate of human technological progress spanning throughout the entire Stone Age period.

Archaeologists, generally use the term 'Neolithic' to imply a purely technological rather than an economic phenomenon. Thus, the use of ground and polished tools, pottery and agriculture came to be seen as inextricably linked. Hence, the Neolithic is basically understood as a sub-division of the Stone Age and the stone tools associated with the period, unlike those of the earlier phases, are grounded and polished (Sankalaia, 1962, p.279).

In recent years, there has been a shift in perception of Neolithic and greater emphasis being placed on socio-economic change that took place in the evolution of human culture and has been associated with the beginning of sedentary life, and domestication of plants and animals (Diar, 1988, p.16). Thus, a definition which was conceived purely from a technological basis is too rudimentary to explain the vast dimension of cultural changes that took place during the Neolithic period. For generations, the term Neolithic has been used as a means of describing a variety of different phenomena: tools, practices, animals, monuments or people. There is a strong desire among archaeologist to come up with a clearer definition as to what actually constitute a Neolithic society, and how it can be represented as a coherent entity determined by a single historical or evolutionary process. In the light of such argument, the following definition spelled out a clear illustration about the Neolithic;

"The shift in the mode of subsistence to agro-pastoral farming remains the only process which is relatively closely defined, geographically widespread and sufficiently archeologically detectable to act as signature of the Neolithic" (Zvelebil, 1996, pp. 323-325).

The pace of development which took place during the Neolithic was revolutionary to human mode of cultural-material progress (Childe, 1936, p.241). The term 'Neolithic Revolution' received additional meaning from the post-processualist, who has defined the Neolithic as the period when people were *being tamed* and *domesticated,* not only mechanically, but metaphorically (Hodder, 1996, p.243). But the greatest change witnessed during the Neolithic period was that human settlement and domestication of animals have been identified through the conceptual separation of the house from the untamed world. The building of stable houses, the aggregation and even delimitation of settlement, the more elaborate and cultural treatment of the dead, is a clear and secure separation of the domestic from of the wild (Hodder, 1987, pp. 43-56).

Chronology

The transition to agriculture—and to settled village life—occurred at different times in various parts of the world. The Neolithic period made its first appearance at the end of the Pleistocene period where the first evidence of human exploitation of the wild precursors of domesticated sheep, goat and cattle were reported from the sites of the Indo-Iranian, notably from the caves in the valleys of the Hindu kush (site of Aq Kupruk) dating to the period of 7000-10,000 years ago (Allchin and Allchin, 1989, p.97).

Plant domestication on the other hand, emerged from foraging economies in many parts of the world during the early Holocene period (12000-10000 years ago). In south western and south eastern Asia, Mesoamerica and South America, seed producing and starchy root plant were brought under human care and propagation by 10000 to 8000 years ago. But because the archaeological records of vegetables and fruits were impoverished by preservation problems, the chronology and location of domestication for some of our modern food is still unknown (Harris, 2000, p.13).

Within the Indian subcontinent, the Neolithic transition did not occur simultaneously across the entire region; rather, Neolithic 'pockets' developed at different point of time in certain key areas within the subcontinent (Barum, 2007, p.65). On the basis of the stray carbon dating from the aceramic stratum of the site of Aq Kupruk-II in northern Afghanistan, the Neolithic period in the sub continent goes back to 10000 BC. In the Indian mainland, Neolithic culture was recognized by around 7000-5000 B.C. where traces of sedentary settlement, was established in the Indus basin, as evident from the site of Mehrgarh (Period I). Neolithic cultures did not appear in other region of the subcontinent before 4000 B.C (Habib, 2001, pp.56). In northern India, the earliest signs of Neolithic appeared at around 2800-2500 B.C. on the basis the aceramic culture from the site of Burzahom in the Kashmir valley. The carbon dating of Kodekal and Utnur reveal an entirely indigenous Neolithic culture which appeared in

the South India around 3000 B.C. and lasted till about 2100 B.C. In the north east India (which will be dealt separately in the next paragraph), survey-explorations and few excavation, have brought of Neolithic culture across the region.

For a long time, the Neolithic cultures of North East India have been associated with those of South West China and South East Asia. This is due to fact that much of the Neolithic activities of North East India bear the Neolithic trademarks of South East Asia and South West China (Sankalaia, 1962, p.297). From the evidence of mainland sites of South East Asia, Chester Gorman made a general review showing that the initial date of the Hoabinhian occupation might be placed at 13000-14000 B.P. and the period between 12000-2000 B.C. witnessed a shift in subsistence base from hunting, gathering to cereal agriculture (*Ibid*) South East Asia was earlier thought to be the cultural backwater with little innovation until the Chinese and Indian influence became instrumental in the development of the Funan and Khmer states in the historic period (Hingham, 1972, p.454). As far as the Neolithic revolution in South East Asia is concerned, the reports from the Sprit caves in North East Thailand have established through excavations, the stratigraphic context of the Neolithic level. The excavation has revealed five superimposed natural and cultural layers with the latest layer was dated to 6000 B.C. Potteries decorated with cord impression and grounded Neolithic stone implements like polished adzes and bifacial knives began to make their appearance from about 7000 B.C. suggesting a strong economic change. Evidence from this site clearly suggest that food plants as well as other botanical remains like gourds, nuts, pepper, and broad beans were found to have been cultivated and not collected. The evidences from Thailand are of great importance, as they have helped to reveal that horticultural activity in South East Asia had started very early (Hingham, 1972, p.461) The earliest evidence of cultivated rice (Oryza *sativa*) in South East Asia was also reported from the Spirit cave and the C[14] dates of rice sample placed the date of the site to 6600 B.C. and 5500 B.C. (Sorenson, 1988). From North East India, the C-14 dates from the site of Khas-

Kalanpur which also yielded microlithic tools along with Neolithic implements has been dated to 1500 B.C. (Sharma, 1991, p.52)

History of Neolithic Studies in North East India

The earliest reported archaeological investigation in the North Eastern parts of India that proved the existence of prehistoric remains in the region goes way back to year 1867 (Lubbock, 1867, p.822). The region is considered to be archaeologically as *terra incognita in* spite of its potential as the area for the domestication of variety of food vegetation. When A.H. Dani (Dani, 1960, p.42) used the term 'Neolithic' for the stone implements collected from Northeast India that are housed at the Pitts Rivers Museum, Oxford, it was not readily accepted by earlier scholar(s) like Allachin, since no potteries were reported in association with stone tools (Sankalia, 1962, p.285). It was only when pottery was found in association with the ground and pecked tools, that use of the term became justified (*Ibid*). It is however not a misnomer to associate the term 'Neolithic' for the Northeastern stone implements, since potteries cannot be the only measuring index for the presence of Neolithic culture in the region. Ethnographic studies clearly reveal that bamboo and other vegetative products are extensively used by the people of the region for storing and even cooking purposes, to the extent that, these material could have easily been supplements to potteries, at least during the early phase of the Neolithic cultural stage in the region.

Following John Lubbock's report, there were sporadic finds of smooth stone tools from different parts of the north-eastern region by E.H. Steel (Steel, 1870, pp. 267-68), Barron (Barron, 1872, pp. 62-63) and Godwin-Austin (Godwin-Austin, 1875, p.158). H.C. Dasgupta was the first among the local investigators who made a report about the discovery of two shouldered tools from Assam (Gupta, 1913, pp. 291-94). The first systematic classification of tools from North East India was attempted by Coggin Brown (Brown, 1917, pp. 130-33) in 1917. J.H. Hutton (Hutton, 1928, pp. 228-29) also made a systematic study on the collection from the Naga Hills. He made a classification of three main types of tools from the region and categorised them as; Triangular, Rectangular and Shouldered. Hutton even attempted to correlate the affinity of the Triangular type with those types that were found in Peninsular India and the Shouldered types with those discovered in Burma and beyond. Although, his work lacks technological details, his effort is not without any significance. In 1929, J.P. Mills (Mills and Hutton, 1929, pp. 295-298) and J.H. Hutton made sketches of six Neolithic tools (three of them shouldered tools) and developed a theory that the shouldered varieties of stone tools derived their origin from metal types which they encountered on their visit to the Naga hills or the small Khasi hoes which were used for cultivation of sweet potatoes. E.C. Worman (Worman, 1949, pp. 181-200) paid special attention to the Neolithic condition of Assam with a view to substantiate his theory of the eastern Asiatic origin of the Neolithic Celt.

In 1949-1959, a typological study was made on 132 Neolithic tools from the eastern and northeastern parts of Assam and Garo hills (64 tools came were collected from the surface of Rongram area in Garo hills) (Goswami, et.al., 1959, pp. 313-14). The author(s) found that the tools from the Kamrup collection are made of slaty shale and compact clay material while those from Garo hills are made of dolerite, quartzite and fine grain granite. They have even speculated that celts made from softer material like clay and slate are not suitable for use and may have ritual origin (*Ibid*).

On the basis of the materials housed at the Pitt Rivers Museum, (Dani, 1960, p.42), claimed that the Neolithic pattern of Assam can be studied on a regional basis. The author claimed that the technique of tool manufacturing is common through out the region with only a slight variation in features. The regional identity is however clearly distinguishable by the raw materials used for making tools. On the basis of typology, Dani, classified the tools into seven classes (1)Type A-Facetted Tool (2)Type B-Rounded-Butt Axe (3)Type C-Axe with Broad cutting edge (4)Type D-Splayed Axe (5)Type E-Shouldered Tool (6)Type F&G-Tanged Axe and

Wedge-Blades and (7)Type H-Grooved Hammer-Stones. He further argued that the square cut forms, recovered from the region was obtained using a wire cutting method (he meant metal wire) and postulated that they are the stones copies of metal prototypes (*Ibid*, p.225). This idea was however refuted by T.C. Sharma on the ground that the wire-saw implies a much higher level culture than what the tools reflect. Instead, the latter, suggested that a sliver of bamboo with sand as an abrasive material, was enough to produce the tang of the rectilinear shouldered axes (Sankalaia, 1961, p.297).

The first regular exploration and excavation in the region was conducted by M.C. Goswami and T.C. Sharma and a team from the University of Guwahati at the site of Daojali Hading (Bhuyan, 1993, pp. 34-35) in North Cachar Hills, during two seasons of systematic excavation between 1961 and 1963. According to the excavators, the site yielded a four cultural sequence described as 1.Hoabinhian 2.Early Neolithic 3.Late Neolithic and 4.Aneolithic. The Neolithic deposit consisted of corded ware pottery, shouldered celts, miniature quadrangular rounded celts of the Belan type, splayed axes and chisels. A total number of 212 numbers of stone implements (65 from excavations, 60 from road cuttings and 77 from the surface of the site) and over 600 sherds were collected from the site. The stone implements were mostly made of shale and sandstone (Sankalia, 1962, p.296). According to H.D. Sankalia, the most important contribution of T.C. Sharma was 'the systematic classification of the entire Assamese collection taking into consideration the sub-marginal features, and the part played by the raw materials. On technological grounds, the Neolithic of Assam included three large groups of stone tools 1.Edge Ground stone implements 2.Pecked and edge ground stone implements and 3.Fully ground implements. He also pointed out the affinity of the Assamese with the Peninsular on one hand and the South-east Asian on the other'. Although no radio metric date has been assigned to the cultural materials from Daojali Hading, the excavator(s) tentatively dated the Neolithic phase of the site to 5000-2000 B.C. (Sharma, 2002, p.475).

T.C. Sharma also attempted a systematic classification of the Neolithic potteries of Assam and divided the pottery collection recovered from the site of Daojali Hading into four groups of wares; 1.Cord-marked 2.Incised 3.Stamped and 4.Plain fine red ware pottery (Sharma, 1967, pp. 126-128).

Other excavations in the region was conducted by S.N.Rao between 1971-74 at the two sites of Sarataru and Marakdola situated in the area bordering the Khasi hills on the south and Kamrup District on the North (Rao, 1977, pp. 191-205). From a 33cm thick single cultural deposit, the Neolithic site of Sarutaru revealed evidences of ground stone tools made of slate of dark grey colour and sandstone of cream to buff colour. The tools were classified as shouldered and round-butted. Hand-made potteries of brown and grey varieties with patterns such as (a) simple cord impressions (b) twisted cord impressions (c) herringbone patterns and (d) zig-zag patterns were found by the excavator. From the post-Neolithic site of Marakdola, the excavator collected archaeological materials in three layers measuring to a maximum depth of 60 cm. The cultural materials from this site included wheel made pottery, a shouldered celt and terracotta objects. Layer 3 of the site has been dated by C-14 dating to 658±93 years B.P. that is 1292 A.D.

The North Eastern Neolithic; its Origin, Divergence and Cultural Affinity

E.C. Worman believed that the smooth stone celts of the 'Neolithic' appear to have been derived from the eastwards, as the eastern part of India fairly belonged to the South and East Asiatic area throughout which the evolution of the post-pleistocene prehistoric cultures were more or less similar (Dani, 1960, p.223). The Neolithic evidences that have been reported from the North eastern region of India so far are generally linked with those of China and South East Asia and not with the Indian sub-continent. The shouldered celts and the cord-impression wares which are typical to the Neolithic culture of the region probably originated from the Lungshoinoid farming culture of China which was developed prior to the Shang period in the

16

beginning of the 2nd millennium B.C. and from where it was believed to have spread gradually into South China, South East Asia and beyond (Clark, 1969, pp. 225-227). But against the generally accepted view, T.C. Sharma supported the view of Colani that the shouldered axes were not derived from the Shang dynasty of North China, but have more affinity with the Hoabinhian culture whose proto-type are the naturally occurring pebble (Sankalaia, 1962, p.298).

The shouldered celts and the facetted ground stone axe are the characteristic tools of the Eastern Indian Neolithic which also include the cord-marked grey ware pottery. These artefacts are widely distributed across Bihar, Orrisa, Bengal and Assam. According to Dani, the shouldered tool type came to Assam through Cachar hills zone from Burma. In the interior it degenerated into irregular variety as in the Khasi hills, Brahmaputra valley and Garo hills zone, and this irregularity suggested that they are the rough copies of the original specimens (Dani, 1960, p.76).The source of this technology is from Sichuan in south China, where the fully developed shouldered axe and cord-marked ware (found in pre-Neolithic contexts) had already appeared right from the Mesolithic phase (Driem, 1998, p.72). H.D. Sankalia believed that the Neolithic of North East India drew their inspiration from Southwest China and Indo-China and the major role was played by the upper Yangtze valley of Szechwan and Yunnan in developing the Neolithic of the region. He further showed that the 'pecked' and 'edged' ground axes and jadeite axes of Naga Hills were introduced into the region from China (Sankalaia, 1962, p.297).

While tracing the origin of the Eastern Indian Neolithic, it is valuable to bring in the Linguistic hypothesis put forth by George Van Driem;

The manufacturing techniques characteristics of the Indian Eastern Neolithic were introduced into Eastern India by the Western Tibeto-Burmans speakers who are technologically more superior than, the presumably Austro-Asiatic speakers whom they met with and with whom they mingled in the process of migration. These Neolithic technologies were adopted by the Austro-Asiatics who came to master the technique, albeit imperfectly. In fact the Austro-Asiatics were held responsible for the spread of Eastern Indian Neolithic technologies in the region as far south west as Orrisa beyond the areas colonised by the ancient western Tibeto-Burmans.

The axe with the broad cutting edge found in the Indian Eastern Neolithic presents technologies which the Austro-Asiatic population already possessed before the advent of the Western Tibeto-Burmans for unlike most of the Eastern Indian Neolithic assemblages, these implements have many parallels in other parts of India (See Fig. 3 Hypothetical Map, courtesy: Geroge Van Driem)[10].

The Neolithic artefacts from the Eastern India are grouped under two heads;

(1) The Bihar-Bengal-Orrisa culture complex

(2) The Assam culture complex.

The first complex represents the typical Indian types while the second complex represents a mixture of foreign types from South East Asia (Dani, 1960, p.223). Although no chronological information has been established till date, but, on the basis of the assumption that manufacturing of shouldered axe required the aid of metal, the Eastern Neolithic was assigned to a relatively later period about the second half of the first millennium B.C. (*Ibid*, p.226). Other archaeologists however, stretch the date of the earliest phase of the Eastern Neolithic to a much earlier period going to the period as early 5000 and 10,000 B.C. (Sharma, 1989, p.59). Till date, the earliest radio metric dating of the Neolithic from North Eastern India comes from the late Neolithic deposit of Khas-Kalyanpur in Tripura where C-14 placed the site to year 1500 B.C. (Sharma, 2002, p.478).

---

[10]In connection with this paper, the author put forth an opinion that the correctness of the hypothesis that ancient Austro Asiactics might have expanded from Southeast Asia cannot be taken for granted.

Factors retarding the progress of Prehistoric studies of North East India

The focus of this investigation is to understand the distribution of Neolithic sites within the Khasi and Jaintia hills of Meghalaya in order to work out the settlement and movement patterns of Neolithic people in these hills. The finding from this research is also expected to throw some light about the region's Neolithic culture and its relation with the Neolithic culture of the neighbouring sites of the Khasi and Jaintia hills. Till date, the Neolithic phase in the area under this research has not received due attention from investigators in spite of the Neolithic evidences found repeatedly. While trying to highlight the present status of Neolithic studies in the region, it is also crucial to understand some of the decisive factors which have probably slowed down the pace of archaeological investigation in the region.

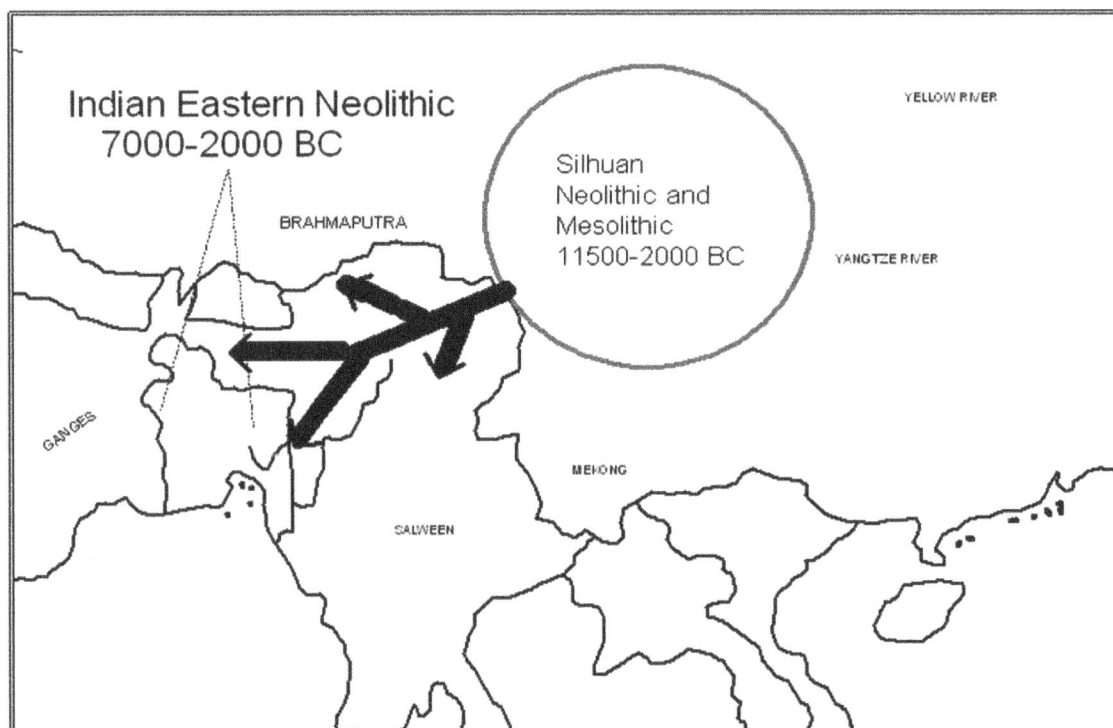

Figure 3: Hypothetical Map of Ancient Tibeto-Burman Migration (Courtesy: George Van Driem)

The moist and humid climatic condition which is not suitable for the preservation of archaeological materials either because of the acidic nature of the soil or the large scale erosion activity which has disturbed both the context and the content of the materials[11] is one of the most discouraging factors for archaeological exploration in the region.

The problem of safety and security is further aggravated by the rise of militancy in the region. In the light of the above mentioned factors, the progress of archaeological investigation in the region would rely heavily upon the initiative taken up by local researchers. The region has great archaeological potential which not only can contribute to the progress of archaeology in India, but of South Asia as a whole, since the region is located on the cultural-transition belt linking mainland India with South East Asia.

---

[11]Firstly this condition speeds up the rate of decomposition of archaeological materials and secondly, the heavy erosion has caused a major displacement of the archaeological material from their original context.

A Brief Review on Archaeological Research in Khasi-Jaintia Hills

Archaeological research in the central Meghalaya plateau especially in the Khasi and Jaintia hills have not been brought to the limelight, in spite of its potential for prehistoric investigation. The discovery of large numbers of Neolithic and pre-Neolithic sites in the adjoining Garo hills (Sharma, 1991, p.49) clearly indicated that there was a possibility of locating similar sites in the Khasi and Jaintia hills also, owing mainly to their geographical proximity from each other. The first reported discovery of Neolithic implements from the Khasi-Jaintia hills dates back to the year 1875 (Godwin-Austin, 1875, P.159) and 1879 (Cockburn, 1879, pp. 133-143). After this initial breakthrough, there was no report of any further discovery of Stone Age implements from the region. Another team of investigators from the Anthropology department of the Gawahati University in 1979 reported about a Neolithic site at Umiam-Barapani which lies in the heart of Khasi hills about 17 kms from the capital of Shillong. Exploration at the site continued till 1995 and various scholars have collected stone implements from the site adding to a total of 84 tools (Hussain, 1996, pp. 111-117). Random surface collections of stone implements were made from the confluence of Umiam and Umshing streams on the eastern edge of the present Barapani Lake below the dam. The artefact assemblages reported from the site included, typical axes, a shouldered celt, flakes and blade tools which are made from indurated shale (Sharma, 1991, p.51). The site has been designated by the investigators as a factory site (Medhi, 1993, p.39). Although quite a fair amount of tools have been collected from the

site of Barapani over the years, no serious attempt has been made to understand the Neolithic culture that flourished at the site which could otherwise help to understand the Neolithic culture of the region under study. In spite of repeated mention of the site in various articles (Medhi, 1990, Sharma, 1991, Bhuyan, 1993) on Northeast prehistory, no effort was made to understand the historical and archaeological relevance of the site. Strictly speaking, the Neolithic culture of the Khasi and Jaintia hills still remained untouched and there is a great potential for archaeological exploration in this region with a scope of generating data about the Neolithic culture of these hills in the context of understanding the man-land relationship.

As far as the excavated sites are concerned, only the site of Sarataru and Marakdola (Roa, 1977) which are located close to the Khasi hills have been systematically studied. The two excavations have provided some information about the Neolithic industry of the region and offer significant insight into the Neolithic culture of the area under study.

The site of Daojali Hading is another important Neolithic site in the context of the area under study. This site is close to the area under study and was subjected to regular excavation, between 1961-1963 in the course of which artifacts recovered from the excavation were clearly recorded and analysed. The site is significant, as it can help to provide some insights into the movement patterns of the Neolithic people in the lower Brahamaputra valley thereby, allowing scope to correlate the relationship with the Neolithic culture of the area under study.

CHAPTER 3

ETHNOARCHAEOLOGY:
Evidences from North East India

Meaning and Concept

The objective of archaeology is to reconstruct the life ways of the people responsible for the archaeological remains (Renfrew *et.al.*, 1991, p.11) and to synthesise the knowledge of human material remains from the past in the context of time and space, in order to recreate the history of man in its true cultural and physical environment (Iyer, 1967, p.2). The subject encompasses a number of different 'archaeologies' which are nevertheless united by the common methods and approaches. The most widely used tools for interpreting archaeological materials is 'analogy' (Ascher, 1961, p.317), a theoretical apparatus by which archaeologists benefit from ethnological knowledge (Chang, 1967, p.229). The studies of contemporary socio-economic behaviour of human groups have therefore come to play a key role in providing such an analogy for archaeological interpretation.

The use of analogy was introduced into archaeology more than a century ago and this can be traced back to the era of classical evolutionary ideology (Stiles, 1977, p.34). Ethnographic study, which is the direct observation of the form, manufacture, distribution, meaning and use of artefacts in their institutional settings, is one such approach which has been used for the purpose of constructing models to aid archaeological analogy and inferences. It has been rightly stated that archaeological reconstruction is an analogy even with or without explicit ethnological recourse (Chang, 1967, p.230).

The recognition for the need of ethnographic material, on which analogies are founded, gave rise to a new sub-discipline called 'Ethnoarchaeology', an approach which grown from the need of archaeologist to look at surviving societies from the point of view of archaeology. The sub-discipline is neither a

theory nor a method, but a research strategy. It embodies a range of approaches both in the living context and to understand archaeological records in order to inform archaeological concepts and to improve interpretation (David *et.al.*, 2001, p.2). This approach emerged as a useful means in the interpretation of archaeological materials, by which contemporary social-cultural behavior is seen from an archaeological perspective (Gould, 1968, p.110). Ethnoarchaeology, as a concept, is sometimes understood differently because its subject matter and aims overlap with some other allied sub-discipline such as 'anthropological archaeology' and 'archaeological ethnography' in terms and approaches. A better understanding of 'Ethnoarcheology' can also be derived from the following definition;

"..the formulation and testing of archeologically oriented and/or derived methods, hypotheses, models and theories with ethnographic data. Ideally one starts with archaeological testing of hypotheses, models and /or theories about those interests and the return to the archeological record to implement the understanding gained from the ethnographic data"(Kent, 1987, p.11).

The term 'Ethnoarcheology' was coined by Jesse Fewkes (Fewkes, 1900, pp. 577-633) to mean an archaeologist *"who can bring as preparation for his work an intensive knowledge of the present life"*. However, the method of ethnoarchaeology was already used by other workers before Fewkes (Cushing, 1886, pp. 467-521). The formal appearance of ethnoarchaeology as a sub-discipline [12] dates back to the year 1956 to a

---

[12]In the new world, 'Ethnoarchaeology', it started as a sub-discipline of Anthropology.

paper written by Maxime Kleindienst and Patty Jo Watson (Kleindienst *et.al.*, 1956, pp. 75-78)[13].

The idea and the name of the sub-discipline is a subject which is still debated. Thus, terms like "Archeoethnography" (Oswalt, 1974, pp. 3-14), was used for obtaining ethnographic information relevant to the interpretation of archaeological finds. Then appeared another term "Living Archeology" (Gould, 1968, pp. 29-48), which means the actual effort made by archeologist to study living communities in order to attain references for archeological patterning, came into use. Ethnoarchaeologists realise the existence of a close interplay between archaeological results and their application to ethnology. It also helps in generating new data in understanding the history of material, cultural elements and the history of ethnic elements and entities (Chang, 1967, p.232).

Types of Ethnoarchaeological Approach

Analogy is the principal theoretical apparatus by which an archaeologist gains ethnological knowledge. Interpretation made through analogy evaluates any belief about non-observed behaviour in reference to observed behaviour which is thought to be relevant (Ascher, 1961, p.317). There are two kinds of analogies commonly employed by the archaeologist:

1) The Direct Historical Analogy: This type of analogy is applied when there is a temporal continuity between the archaeological culture and the ethnographic culture. It is generally considered to provide the highest probability of being correct. Such continuity is based either from historical records and description known as "area historical" or, based on field work in the area under consideration known as "area ethnographic model" (Steward, 1942, pp. 337-343).

(2) General Comparative Analogy: This analogy is based mainly on the similarities between contemporary cultures and the cultural

materials from an archaeological context. In such analogy, correlation between the two sets of cultures can be made on a cross-cultural level without any special restriction (Chang, 1967, p.229).

Ethnoarchaeology and Tradition

While pursuing historical research with an archaeological approach, the ways of life in the contemporary traditional mode can contribute greatly in providing an analogy about the ones in the past, since archaeological interpretation basically depends and ultimately rests on analogy[14]. The significance of ethnology in archaeology can be understood from the conclusion made by some archaeologists that archaeological reconstruction is an analogy with or without ethnological recourse (Chang, 1967, p.230). But as the science of archaeology deals only with the material remains of the past, it becomes a requisite that only such traditions which are manifested in the material content of the society come to occupy a centre stage in its subject matter.

In order to understand the material culture preserved in traditional practices, ethnoarchaeology tries to study the possible correlation between the material culture of the people on one side and the unobservable social relations or spiritual life on the other (Neustupny, 1993, p.168). Thus the material data can be use to integrate knowledge to other non-material facets of the society which are reflected and embedded in tradition through an approach called 'folk archaeology' (Michlovic, 1990, pp. 103-107). In this way, archaeology contributes directly towards historical reconstruction when conventional historical sources are lacking or when other forms of preserved traditions require substantial support. Hence, it helps in reducing the mythical notion about the ancient ways of life, particularly the lifestyle of the pre-historic people.

Most of the preliterate societies developed their own history (oral) and formulated it with a

---

[18]They Invited archaeologist to take to the field of living communities with his own theoretical orientation and gather the necessary information p.77

[14]Held that, if something is like something else in some respect, it is likely to be similar in others.

motive to preserve and transmit ideas (with or without inflating or deflating them) to the later generations. In many cases, societies used (super) natural agents (*not historical theories*) as their scale of references. Generally, in the process of interpreting the traditional history which is not manifested in the material evidence, there is a tendency of over-interpretation on the subject matter. At times, when the investigator is under the influence of the contemporary conditions, the situation may lead to a biased interpretation. For a safer and plausible representation of the traditional interpretation, and to check the flaw of over interpretation, observation of traditions is gauged mainly within the milieu of the material form or those which are manifested in physical attributes. Using this method, oral tradition can become part and parcel of ethnoarchaeological research, not as a partial and fragmentary record of the past, but as true elements that can be rescued from the clouding fantasy and helped to blend the two interacting modes of representing the past by using different accounts of the same events and objects (Layton, 1999, p.31).

The concept of 'Thunder Axe' in North East India

The scope for ethnoarchaeological studies in North East India is quite vast especially given the fact that much of the region is still rural in character and traditional ways of life linger on in almost all aspects of life. Tradition continues to dominate the world view of the people. In the North East India, as well as in general, people cling to tradition either out of fear or reverence or simply by convention, though the intensity of adherence understandably varies from group to group. The process of cultural development is thus keenly visible among the cultures of North East Indian tribes; most of them in some form or the other do retain some fabric of pre-historic life ways. A record of this surviving process can be of great use for extracting information about the past ways of life, even extending to very remote times.

In the context of the North East India, ethnoarchaeology has ample scope as its application in the region expands beyond the understanding of material culture alone. The multiplicity and variety of preserved traditions render the region to be a storehouse of preliterate cultures. Thus, if ethnoarchaeology stresses on observing the ways of the pre-literate people, the traditional practices and belief systems which the tribes in this part of the world have carried with them from generations to generations, it can unfold valuable information about the past and act as an aid to archaeological recourse.

The concept of 'thunder Axe' is one of the many distinctive aspects of ancient belief systems which probably date back to a very remote period. This belief is retained in the form of tradition by almost all the tribes that inhabited the North East region of India. Thus by applying the general comparative analogy for the concept of 'Thunder Axe', great insights could be gained about the cultural and cognitive patterns of prehistoric life.

The Neolithic stone tools, owing to their peculiar nature, have always mystified the common man who cannot diagnose them scientifically. These stone objects are assumed to be material products of thunder and lightning. The notion of a "thunder Axe" became a popular belief which remained unquestioned throughout the world, stretching from Europe, Africa, Asia Minor, India and Far East. Before the introduction of modern archaeology in Korea, prehistoric stone tools were commonly called thunder axes. In China, a thunder axe was seen as a heavenly object having medicinal properties from as early as the 8th c. AD (Seonbok, 2002, p.293).Traditional people believed that these thunder axes can immunize people and property from attack by lightning and thunder (Balfour, 1929, p.46). In Scandinavia and Germany, people would hurl the 'thunderbolt (axe)' against the building, the door or the roof imitating the thunder strike in order to increase the chances of immunity from the real thunder strike. There is no reference about the concept of 'thunder axe' from the mainland of India, although, a picture in one of the reports from Tamil Nadu showed a picture of stone implements being placed at a shrine as objects of worship (Narasimhaiah, 1980, Plate 1 B).

As stated earlier, the various tribes of North East India consider the Neolithic stone tools as 'thunder axe' with magical and medicinal properties. In their local dialects, the following terms are used to denote these objects;

The Kachari tribe of Assam refer to these stones in their local language as *Sarak, ni-Ongthai* (*Sarak*=Heaven, *ni*=of *Ongthai*=stone) (Goswami *et.al.*, 1959, p.313).

In Santhali dialect these stones which came along with a thunder strike are called *Ceter* or thunder Axe. The traditional Sanatal people believe that the stones also have medicinal properties. They would rub the stone on a rough surface and whatever dust particle that comes out of the grinding process is dissolved in water and served as medicine.

The Karbi and Tiwa tribes of Assam call the stones as *Choteracho* meaning thunder stone and they are also said to have magical and religious power with medicinal properties (Medhi, 2002, p.57).

Among the Adi tribe of Arunachal Pradesh, these stones are called *Lidar* which means a thunder stone. Infact no one is allowed to touch these stones because of superstitions that is associated with it.

The Garos of Meghalaya refer to these stones as *Goera gitchi* (Goswami *et.al.*, 1959, p.314). (*Goera*=god of lighting; *gitchi*=hoe[15]).

The Angami Nagas call them *Methie* meaning thunder axe; in the Chongli and Mongsen dialect of the Ao Nagas it is called *Tsungyipo* and *Tsunglaao* respectively, which mean thunder axe. According to J.P. Mills, many of the latter stone implements obtained from the Nagas and Kukis have already been scraped and otherwise damaged because they have been

used as medicines. It is said that the Kukis would Oath in the name of these stone objects (Mills *et.al.*, 1929, p.296).

The Burmese refer to them as *Mo-gyo* meaning sky chain or thunderbolt (Gurdon, 1914, p.12).
The Jamatia tribe of Tripura calls these stones as *Fwirang* or *Pherang* which simply means thunder stones and these objects are often kept close to storage bins of food grains.

The Mizos or Lushai of Mizoram refer to these stones as *Tek* (the term itself means thunder) and the people of this tribe not only consider these stones as implements of their ancestors but also ascribe their origin to a thunder strike.

From the area where the present research is undertaken, the Khasis have also preserved in their tradition the concept of thunder axe and this tradition is still living in many of the rural areas of Khasi and Jaintia hills. In their local dialect, the people refer to these stones as *U Sdie Pyrthat* or the Thunder Axe. The tradition of thunder axe is largely preserved among the Khasi people who inhabit the northern belt of the central and eastern Meghalaya plateau. The physical feature of this region is defined by the undulating hills of south Brahmaputra valley known as the Ri-Bhoi region and those of the northern parts of Jaintia hills bordering the Cachar hills districts. The Bhoi-Khasis as they are commonly known, do not allow the people to keep the thunder axe inside the house for fear that thunder may strike the house or the property. The people of this region and some parts of Jaintia hills also believe that these thunder axes are of two varieties, the '*live axes*' and '*spent axes*'. Their traditional knowledge explains that the black coloured stones are the 'spent' types, while the white coloured ones are the '*live*' types. They also refer to the '*live*' variety are those axes which cannot protect a person or property from the attack of lightning or thunder strike, where as the '*spent*' variety as those which can immunize persons and property from the attack by lightning and thunder. This same belief prevails among the some Naga tribes too.

---

[15] A hoe is a triangular iron leaf-like implement with a slender tenon attached to a wooden handle and this was use for garden cultivation normally in jhum fields (reference: Khasi Hills). (See Plate 21)

In Sutnga, a village in Jaintia hills, which lies on the eastern part of Meghalaya, these thunder axes are still used by local healers as a form of medicine. Like other people around the world and the region, the people of Sutnga would scrape the stones into powder and dissolve them in water and take as medicine (Mitri, 2008, p.224). The people of this village, especially the local healer claimed that the *'spent'* types are those which have no magnetic properties while the *'live'* are those which still retained magnetic pull. Only the *'live'* ones are used for making medicine.

Discussion

The concept of 'thunder axe' is an important ethnographic evidence to help us collect preliminary information on the locations of Neolithic culture or sites in any part of the region. Although the existing traditional idea of thunder axe may not be directly useful for archaeology since much of the information have been clothed in mythical association, a closer examination of the traditional explanation of the Neolithic axes can however, open up new questions to help formulate hypothesis on at least two theoretical conditions;

(i) To establish some form of conjecture about the determining factors which could have probably engendered the rise of such a concept among the traditional people.
(ii) To use the traditional concept in order to achieve some understanding about the dual role of these prehistoric tools, as items of utility and items of symbolic significance.

While dealing with the concept of thunder axe, it appears that much of the subject is closely linked with the evolution of 'religion' itself. But viewed from another perspective, tradition seems to support a model that the important role played by these archaeological materials within the socio-economic system (mainly their functional utility) fostered their evolution into mythical objects attaining symbolic significance. May more speculations can be forwarded to deal with this problem, but for a brief discussion on the topic, the following inter-connected hypothetical questions can be made:

(a) Are these stone tools mistaken for other objects that have real association with the sky, such as the meteorites?
(b) Has their functional utility in the past help to elevate their role to a symbolic and mythical position?
(c) Are the authors of the stone tools culturally separated from those who rendered them into mythical objects?

There is good evidence from Europe that even fossil echinoids (*sea urchins*) were looked upon as thunder bolts. Along with this, the aeroliths or meteoric stones which were also dug up from the soil have added to the theory of the thunder axe (Balfour, 1929, p.39). This seems to explain the hypothetical question no. (a) And it may be speculated that the peculiarity of the stone tools which do not have a natural shape must have indeed generated the concept of a thunder axe.

Balfour in his article observed that, among people like the Tasmanian, the Aborigines of Australia, the Melanesians and Polynesians whose culture have never advanced beyond the stone age, there is little trace of belief in the mystic origin of these stone implements. This observation seems to support and affirm the hypothesis that the authors and the users of the stone tools were indeed culturally separated from those who render them into mythical origin as indicated in the hypothetical question no. (c). But it is not a part of the discussion here to delve into the debate about the spatial and temporal nature of such a cultural separation.

There is an ongoing debate about the way objects come to assume religious and mythical characteristics. Mircea Eliade, while examining the nature of symbolic thinking, believes that most of the things that made up ordinary life are profane; and says that they are just themselves and nothing more, but at a right moment anything profane can be transformed into something more than itself–into 'sacred', which he termed as 'dialectic of the sacred' (Eliade, 1996, pp. 158-197).

Applying Mircea Eliade's model theory of symbolism as analogy, two propositions can be considered with regard to the concept of thunder axe; firstly, it can be explained that, if there existed a cultural or a temporal gap between the users of the stone tools and those who rendered them into mythical objects, then an inference can be made that the concept of thunder axe was unconsciously developed because the purposes of these stone tools remain vague to those who found them. Therefore the elevation of these stone tools into mythical objects was *superficially*[16] developed. This proposition does not support the above model-theory of symbolism. The ethnographic survey from Khasi and Jaintia hills of Meghalaya clearly shows that even the rural people in the present times are ignorant about the origin of such a concept. One thing is however certain, that, in general the Khasi people believe that these stones came down from the sky during the lightning and thunder strike. It is not wrong to speculate that probably the concept of thunder axe may have gained a mythical recognition because the people failed to comprehend the cause of thunder.

Based on the information gathered from elderly people of different Khasi villages, it is observed that at least one factor is responsible for origin of this 'concept'. Ethnographic demonstration explains that when a lightning or thunder strikes, trees get uprooted and this led to a natural process of excavation of the soil. The villagers who subsequently found these axes which are exposed as a result of thunder storm, cause to be called thunder axe. A similar kind of explanation was also speculated by Lt. Barron in his article when he reported about the two Neolithic implements from Naga Hills way back in 1868 (Barron, 1872, p.63). It is quite reasonable hence, to believe that the Neolithic tools with apparently unfamiliar shapes and designs must have created different perspectives in the minds of the preliterate people, and as such concept of 'thunder axe' gained recognition. This, perhaps, was that *'right moment'* when the profane assumed a status of the 'sacred'. In the line of such assumptions, the mythical association of the stone tools is therefore superficially developed.

In the second proposition, an argument may be forwarded that, if there is cultural and temporal continuity between the authors of the stone implements and those who rendered them into mythical objects, then, the evolution of these stone tools from objects of utility into objects of symbolic and religious importance was a process which was *deliberately* adopted. Thus, the mythical notion about the Neolithic stone implements must have emerged consciously owing to their utility factor being rendered sacred out of the profane at some point of time in a constant and recurring pattern throughout the world. The 'Neoliths', which are the harbingers of the beginning of human material abundance were therefore elevated to the mythical realm. Since the physical world is the veritable store house of such symbols, 'thunder', probably became the chosen symbol which offered the preliterate mind the first step of refuge in their search for the supernatural and hence laid the foundation to the beginning of 'religion' itself.

Results Chemical Analysis

In order to generate some inputs into the chemical constituents of the tools and also to assess the presence of any common compounds which may contain medicinal properties of some form or the other, a preliminary test of the patina scrape out from two samples of Neolithic axes (one grey and one black in Colour) from the site of Umiam-Barapani was sent for analysis using a simple IR Spectrum analysis at the Laboratory of the department of Chemistry-North Eastern Hill University (Figures 4, 5 and 6).

---

[16] Italics added to denote the kind of condition that led to rise of such belief.

25

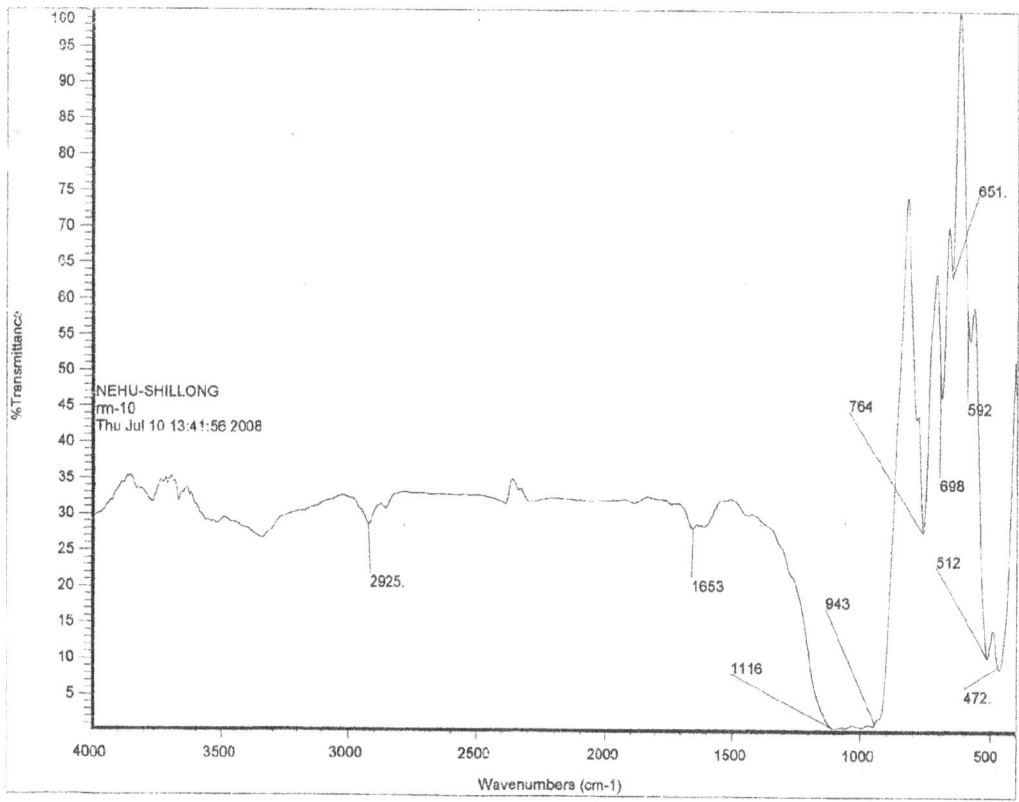

Figure 4: Infrared Spectrum of Sample rm10

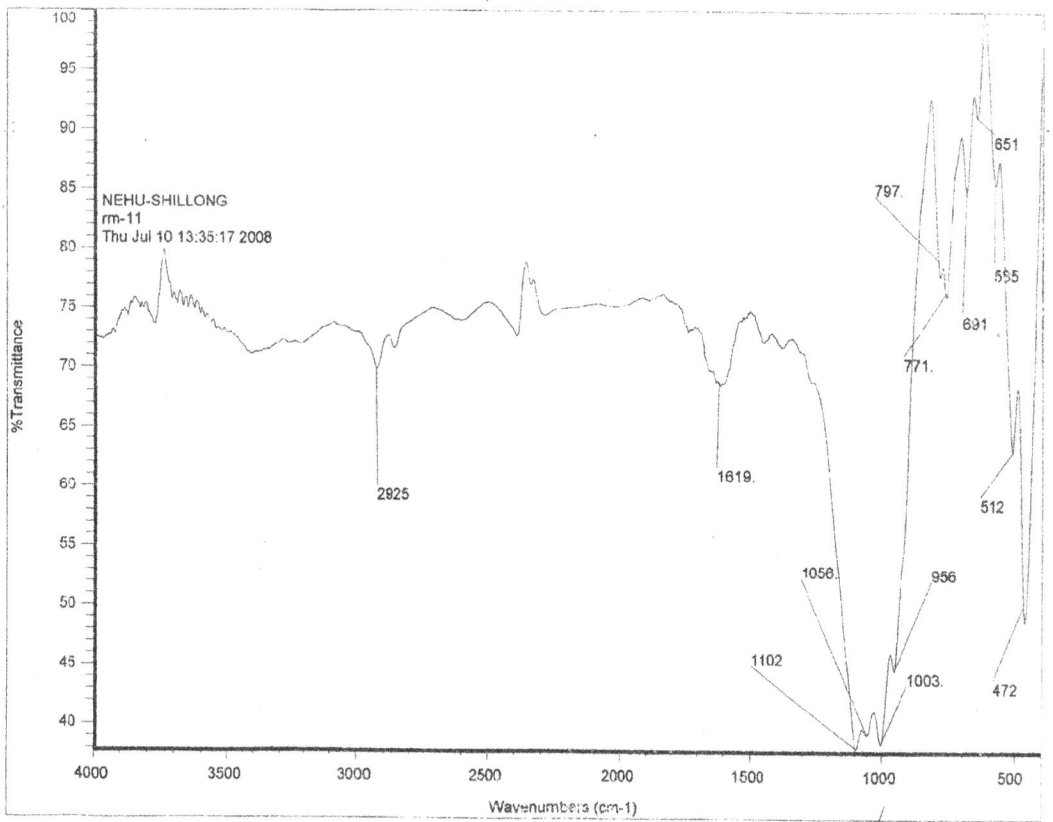

Figure 5: Infrared Spectrum of Sample rm11

<u>Infrared Spectrum of the Sample rm-11</u>

From the infrared spectrum the band assignment are as follows:

- A weak band at 3600 cm^{-1} is due to υO-H.
- Two bands of medium intensity at 2925 cm^{-1} could be assigned to the stretching and rocking modes of H_2O.
- Sharp band at 1100^{-1} is due to the stretching frequencies of SiO_2
- Medium to sharp bands between 771cm^{-1} and 470 cm^{-1} is due to Metal Oxygen stretching frequencies.

<u>Results</u>: **$Al_2O_3.2SiO_2.2H_2O$** (Aluminum Silicate)

The general result from both samples **(rm-11 and rm-10)**[17] in the spectra analysis shows the presence of probably **Metal-Sulphate/Silicate/Aluminium**, without any trace organic constituents.

Reference:

1) Dr. Ashish Malhotra (Union Christian College), Meghalaya.
2) Mr. Rudolf Manih Research Scholar Department of Chemistry. NEHU.

Figure 6: Analysis of Infrared Spectrum

CHAPTER 4

CONTEXTUALISING FOLK TRADITION AND ARCHAEOLOGY:
Evidences from Khasi Hills

Oral tradition in Area of Study

Folklore and oral tradition in the area under study are also taken as one set of evidences to support archaeological sources, especially when both the evidences occurred within the same geographical context. The rich repository of oral traditions can help in enhancing and strengthening the archaeological finds and hence, they are taken as one of the reliable ethno-archaeological sources. In the area under study, there are traces of folk stories which appropriate the archaeological findings, and such stories have been documented to provide additional sources in understanding settlement patterns.

Below are given some important folk stories whose content are linked with the ancient settlement of the Khasi people further strengthened by archaeological finds:

Records of Folk Lore of *Sohpet Bneng* Hill

The folktales associated with *U Sohpet Bneng* have been transmitted orally in different versions, some of which are inflated with stories from other folktales of the Khasi hills.

The first version of the story was recorded by Gurdon (Gurdon, 1914, pp. 173-174);

In the olden days when the earth was very young, they say that Heaven and Earth were very near to one another, because the navel string of Heaven drew the earth very close to it. This navel string resembling the flesh, linked the hill near Sumer with Heaven. At that time all the subjects of the Syiem of Mylliem throughout his kingdom came to one decision i.e. to sever the navel string from that hill. After they had cut it, the navel string became short; and, as soon as it shortened, Heaven then ascended high. It was from that time that Heaven became so high, and it is for that reason that they call the Hill U Sohpet Bneng (Sic).

Another version of the folk story as recorded by a local scholar Hommiwell Lyngdoh (Lyngdoh, 1962, pp. 23-25);

In the ancient times when the Earth was ideal and peaceful, the Khasis were in the beginning composed of U Hynniewtrep and Khyndaiskum (lit. the seven Huts and Nine Nests or huts) and lived in the abode of God. Gradually, seven of the sixteen huts began to learn how to cultivate crops and came down to this earth for cultivation after which they would returned back to their dwellings through the tree which served as a ladder to heaven. The peaceful life continued until one day when the humans chopped off the tree that served as a ladder. From that time the seven huts were stranded in this earth and the nine huts on Heaven. God however had pity on the seven huts and he taught them the art of sowing crops according to seasons, and showed them how to sow the right crop for a good harvest. In the same way God also taught the humans about the rules and regulation to be followed in their life time until they return back to His abode. God finally disappeared from the sight of his people and he can speak to them only through signs and symbols.

The *Sohpet Bneng* hill, essentially, came to occupy a very important position in the history and culture of the people. The Khasi people considered the hill to be the kernel of their culture. The hill was sanctified right from the ancient times[18]. An annual thanksgiving festival known as *Leh Niam SohpetBneng* was revived by the Seng Khasi, an indigenous socio-religious organization in the year 2000 A.D., to preserve the ancient belief that is so closely attached to the genesis of the Khasi community with the Sohpet Bneng hill. The religio-historical status,

---

[18] Remains of an ancient altar of stones which are piled up in pyramidal shape, was reported by an exploration team from *Seng Khasi* in 1989 and this is published in D.L. Nongbri in a local pamphlet. Ka Seng Khasi Bad U Lum Sohpet Bneng. *Ka Lyngkhuh Snem Ba Shispah* 2000. Seng Khasi. Shillong.

assumed by the hill in the assemblage of Khasi folklores, is a topic of great interest for debate and conjectures. An ethnographic and archaeological survey of the surrounding areas in close proximity with the apex of the hill has helped to throw up some form of archaeological data to establish the antiquity and historical processes associated with the folklore.

Etymologically, the word *Sohpet* in the Khasi dialect literally translated as 'Navel' is attached closely with a meaning designating 'the origin' or connection to the 'Beginning' or 'the Root'. The word Bn*eng* literally translated as 'Heaven' denotes 'an ideal state'. It is however understood that only a detailed research on the folktale could bring to light the nature, the content and the general analogy underlying the story of *U Sophet Bneng* in the context of other Khasi folktales. But on the basis of the fundamental background of the folktale, it is apparent that the story of *U SohpetBneng* has some connection with the early history and the initial stages of development of the Khasi society in general, and the historical antiquity of the settlement around the hill or its surrounding areas, in particular.

Although the story associated with *U SopetBneng* hill is shrouded in the form of myth and folklore and cannot be literally historical in nature, it is still incorrect to conclude that this folk narrative has no historical value whatsoever. The kernel of the folk story does carry with it, elements of embedded historical narration of a very long term perspective. Hence, the historicity of the folk story, unlike other historical evidences can be accepted in the form of a compressed narration describing a long term historical process. Additional filtration of the existing story would yield more information to establish its historical authenticity. Such an interpretation is however heavily dependent on other sources of evidences which can provide support in order to establish a hypothesis of an embedded historical narrations of the folk story.

During the course of this research, archaeological explorations were conducted in and around the area of Sohpet Bneng hill in order to establish some correlations between folk narrations and archaeological evidence. The field explorations brought to light evidences of Megalithic monuments and cists or *Mawshyieng*[19], rows of standing menhirs alongside dolmens, five rectangular royal funeral pyre mounds or *Kpep* measuring 6x3meters more or less. A secondary type of Iron smelting area with debris of iron slag was also discovered from an area, including slag pieces from the same site (Mitri, 2004 pp. 68). Further exploration of the site led to the discovery of eight numbers of Neolithic stone tools and few fragmentary pieces of coarse hand-made potsherds. The stone tools were found exposed on the surface of a cultivated field. Although, the original context of the tools have been partially disturbed because of the cultivation process going on in the area, but, they have not shifted much from their original location as all of them are dispersed within an approximate distance of only 10-20 sq.mts (Mitri, 2005, p.90). The tools found from this site are included in the chapter dealing with classification of artefacts from the area under the present research. Some ceramic materials in the form of broken potteries were also recovered from the site along with the stone tools and they are in a fragmentary state. All the pottery samples were hand-made and are burnt at a very low temperature as evident from the bigger space of the dark core at the section profile of the potsherds.

Records of the Folk Lore of *U Lum Diengiei*

The folktale of *Ka Lum Diengiei* (*Lum*=Hill, *Dieng*=Tree) is another oral tradition which occupies a pedestal position among the oral narratives of the Khasi people and on the basis of its content it appears to be connected with a primeval socio-economic cultural setting. The folk lore brings out an interesting narrative

[19]Here post-cremated bones are generally stored inside an earthen pot.

29

about the transition of the society from one socio-economic stage into another. The Diengiei hill lies on the western side of the Umiambarapani lake and rises abruptly towards the West Khasi hill plateau. This oral tradition is amplified in this research mainly because it is associated with a particular area where traces of Neolithic artefacts have been recovered in large numbers. Neolithic evidences were collected from the entire western foothills of Diengiei hill stretching to about 5 kilometers. It is therefore considered necessary to describe this oral tradition in the light of the archaeological findings and established some sort of a direct historical analogy by adopting the "area ethnographic model" (Steward, 1942, pp. 337-343), thereby linking the traditional narrative with the archaeological evidences from the same spatial context.

Gurdon in his records of the Khasi folktales listed in his monograph narrates the following story about "U Lum Diengiei";

Diengiei is one of the highest peaks in the Khasi country resembling in height and size, the Shillong "Peak" which lies opposite and to the north of it. There are many villages on this hill belonging to the Shillong Syiem (chief). In olden days, on the top of this hill grew a gigantic tree overshadowing the whole world, the name of that tree was "Ka Diengiei". The Khasis came to a determination that if this tree were cut down (lit. Destroyed), the world would become good and would have light, for as long as it remain standing (the tree), the world remain dark and unfruitful. They accordingly came to a unanimous decision to fell it. When they cut (the tree) during the day and went back next morning, they found that the marks of cutting had been obliterated. Thus they cut each day, and next morning they found that the marks had disappeared. This was the case always. Then they marvelled why this thing was thus. They asked question and they investigated; 'ka Phriet' (a very small bird) said "all this have happened because a tiger comes every night to (the foot of) the tree and licks the part of the tree which has been cut"[20]. Thereupon, the men having

plied their axes and knives the whole day cutting the tree (instead of carrying them away as usual) tied them to the incision with their edges pointing upwards. So when the tiger went as usual at night to lick the incisions, with their edges pointing outwards, the sharp blades of the axes and knives cut his tongue. Thenceforth, the tiger ceased to go to the tree, and as the tiger ceased to lick the incisions, the mark was not obliterated as before. So their work went on progressing every day until the 'Diengiei' fell. Thus the world received light and cultivation throve, and there was nothing more to stand in the way of the light of the sun and the moon. It was for that reason that the name of "U Lum Diengiei" was given to the hill. Nobody knows what became of the tree, for since the time it fell, its species has died out and there is no seed of it (to be found) anywhere on the earth from which it can be grown" (sic).

An ethnographic record collected from the local people, who live in the villages around the fertile valley called *Ka Sung*, provides additional insights into the folk story of *"Ka Diengiei"*. According to this version, the *Sung* or the fertile valley which geographically stretches along the northern reaches of the Umiam stream right to the border of Jaintia hills is actually a depression created artificially by the branches of *"Ka Diengiei"* tree after it was felled from the top of the Diengiei hill. The *Sung* is known for its fertility and its long stretches of paddy fields can be seen even today along this entire valley.

The folk story of *Ka Diengiei* appears to be a folk narrative which represents the period of transition between the untamed and tamed landscape and probably records the beginning and spreading of agriculture, with the area surrounding Diengiei hill as the area of attraction. Taking into consideration the type of agricultural practices in the region even till today, the story may have close connection with the incipient stage of agriculture. Certain characters mentioned in the folk tale such as 'gigantic tree' and the 'tiger' can be explained as symbolic representation of the forested landscape and its wild habitat. On the basis of the story, it may be speculated that the effort

---

[20]Another version of the story narrates that, a *Phriet* or the small bird (which generally forage near human habitation) agreed to share the secret with the

humans only if they promise to allow it to feed on the grains from their fields after the harvest is done.

made by the people to cut off the gigantic tree thus reflects the process taming the forest with primitive tools in order to clear the dense vegetation for agricultural purposes. Turning to another character in the story, the *Phriet* or the small bird is usually found to forage in open spaces such as paddy fields and other cultivated areas. These birds are mostly found not very far from the human settlement and in the villages of Khasi and Jaintia hills they are trapped by local people and caged as pets in their houses till today. It is also quite apparent from the folk tale, that, this small bird must have assumed a semi-domesticated status from that time onwards as it thrived in open spaces close to human habitat. Its willingness to share the secret with the human to cut down the tree (to clear the forest) supports such an interpretation. This folk tale thus, provides strong clues to the stage of society representing the beginning and spread of agriculture resulting from the clearance of the forested landscape. In this context, it is definitely closely linked with the Neolithic society in these hills.

The ethnographic parallel from the *sung* valley helps to corroborate the folk tale of *Ka Diengiei* whose branches are said to have formed the fertile valley. This parallel story may represent the stage when agriculture began to expand beyond the area of attraction or the foothills of *U Diengiei*. This can be referred to as an inflated version of the original folk tale created perhaps by the movement of the people along the *Sung* valley. The concentration of agricultural activity both in the form of paddy field and hill slopes cultivation continue to flourish throughout the entire *Sung* valley even today.

The findings of Neolithic evidences along the foothills of the Diengiei add further importance to the folk tale as conditioned by their similar spatial context. In fact the archaeological finds from the slopes of the Diengiei hill and its close proximity with Umiam-Barapani site, represents the most complex types of stone implements of Neolithic origin so far not recovered from any of the sites in the entire Khasi and Jaintia hills. The site of Umiam-Barapani is potentially the biggest Neolithic site in the area of attraction in the context of the entire region under study. The location of the site in close proximity with the geographical space of the folk story indirectly seems to establish the relationship between the two, with consideration to the fact that the content of the folk story was also linked with the beginning of domestication of plants and animals. Using Julian Steward's model, this folk lore can be of great use to support the archaeological finds from the area.

Chapter 5

CLASSIFICATION OF NEOLITHIC ARTEFACTS FROM KHASI –JAINTIA HILLS

Plan of Study

The Khasi and Jaintia hills, which encompasses the central Meghalaya plateau is the focus of this investigation. Field work was conducted on selected areas of these hills. The Neolithic artefacts collected during the course of this field work are typologically classified according to their respective shape, form and raw materials. Using the evidence recorded during the course of this research with those that have already been reported from other areas close to the Khasi and Jaintia hills[21], an effort was made in this research to postulate on the movement patterns of Neolithic people within this micro-environment. Other forms of archaeological evidences such as the megalithic monuments and iron slag which do not conventionally fall within the Neolithic stratum are also included to corroborate the Neolithic evidences. Relevant ethnographic data supportive of the archaeological evidence has also been included. The region's environmental system and its relationship with the distribution of Neolithic settlements is also briefly discussed with the objective of gaining some insight about the role of environment in the development of the Neolithic culture of these hills. The following environmental parameters are taken as basic indices to formulate such a relationship:

The Physiographic Parameters (Sharma, 2003, pp. 17-21): (Figure 2)

1. The undulating hills of the north which gradually slopes down towards the Brahmaputra valley and forms the sub-montane region with contour lines between 150-1000 meters above the sea level. This part encompasses the major part of the Ri-Bhoi district of Meghalaya.

2. The Central upland zones of Meghalaya which lies between the contour level of 1200-1500 meters above the sea level. This part covers the major part of the East and West Khasi and Jaintia hills districts of Meghalaya.

3. The precipitous zone of the central southern Meghalaya. This forms the steepest parts of the region and is known as the *war* country. Due to extremely heavy rainfall, the area has been subjected to fluvial erosion. A major part of this zone is located in the East Khasi hills district of Meghalaya.

Climatic Parameters:

1. The Moist-Humid climate type of northern *Ri-Bhoi* and southern *War* region

2. Temperate climate type of Shillong plateau and Jaintia hills

3. Cold climate type of upper Shillong and West Khasi hills.

Field Method

New archaeological insights into the Stone Age cultural phase of the otherwise neglected part of the region has been discovered from four seasons of field work conducted across the Khasi hills, the Ri-Bhoi region, some parts of the West Khasi hills and the Northern tract of Jaintia hills. The substantial archaeological evidences achieved from the field works offer some insights for understanding the distributions of Neolithic sites in this part of Northeast India.

Since archaeological investigation concerning the Stone Age phase in the region is still at its

---

[21]Neolithic materials from the site of Doajali Hading in North Cachar Hills of Assam,Garo Hills of Meghalaya and the site of Sarataru and Marakdola of Assam.

preliminary stage, the present investigation adopted field method where regional parameters are duly considered. Keeping in view the ethnographic population and their environment, the first phase of the field survey was randomly selected on the basis of information received from the reports of local people.

The methods adopted in the course of research and while conducting field work across the region are as follows:

• The first priority was given to areas which are geographically considered to be relatively closer to the already reported Neolithic sites, such as;

    (i) The Northeastern tract of Jaintia Hills, bordering the excavated Neolithic site of Daojali Hading which is located in the North Cachar hills of Assam.

    (ii) The Northern parts of the Ri-Bhoi district of Meghalaya, geographically closest to the excavated Neolithic site of Sarutaru and Marakdola which are located in the Karbi Anglong district of Assam.

    (iii) Parts of West Khasi hills, considered to be important for its geographical proximity to the Garo hills from where Neolithic evidences have been reported in large numbers.

• The second priority in field investigation was given to those areas lying along the course of the major rivers and streams of the region, such as the Umiam and Umkhen river of the Khasi hills and Ri-Bhoi region and the Kynshi river in the West Khasi hills.

• The Valley which is located between the Khasi and Jaintia upland zones was also selected for field survey to understand the adaptation pattern of Neolithic folks in the region.

• Information from local people formed another important source for locating sites

based on the identification of the traditional names of the Neolithic tools.

• The Khasi oral tradition preserved in the form of folktales, myths and legends were also considered during the preliminary stage of field survey. Those stories which are closely linked with the ancient habitation of the people have helped in furthering field investigation and locating pre-historic data. In short, all oral traditions which could help to generate a 'direct historical analogy' from the region have been considered in this investigation.

• The Megalithic monuments[22] found scattered in different places of the Khasi and Jaintia hills are another form of archaeological evidence which indicates the presence of settlements in the past. These monuments served as valuable index for initiating field exploration in locating Neolithic sites.

4. Nature of Finds

The Neolithic finds are mostly artefacts of surface collection with very few of them coming from less-disturbed contexts. The position of some Neolithic sites recorded in this work as factory sites offer potential for more in-depth archaeological investigation in the future. There are also some sites which showed clear continuity (may not be in stratigraphic sense)[23] in the cultural materials belonging to both the Neolithic phase and to the phase when evidence of iron began to appear. This indicates the change and continuity of settlement pattern in the study region spanning from the pre-historic to the historic period.

All the Neolithic artefacts, catalogued in this research as classified under the table below,

---

[22]Only those monuments that appeared to be older were considered.

[23]Although the evidence of cultural continuity from the sites of Sohpet Bneng, San Mer, Umjajew etc. are not observed on the basis of stratigraphic context, the continuity is however apparent when the archaeological evidences are corroborated with other sources of information such, as the oral history.

have been assigned to the respective villages from where they have been collected. The villages, having such reported artefacts, are designated as separate site in this classification. Following the classification made by earlier scholars (Dani, 1960), the tools from the study region are grouped into four types.

On the basis of the shape and possible functions of the working edge the tools are classified as follows:

Type-1. Axe (Plate19.A/B): This class includes all the tools having median working edge produced through equal bifacial grinding. It comprises of tools with rounded, pointed or narrow butt, but shows absolutely no trace of shoulders in any form.

Type-2. Adze (Include chisel) (Plate19.C): It refers to the tools with a beveled working edge, produced either through unequal bifacial or unifacial grinding. At times, some tools display slight trace of shoulders.

Type-3 Shouldered Tools (Plate 20.A): It includes all the tools having clear shoulders with a prominent tenon.

Type-4 Tanged Tools (Plate 20.B): The tools in this class have a small tenon with no proper angle between the tenon and the sides.

Miscellaneous (Plate 18.D): There is also another class of tools termed as 'harvesters' recorded from the areas like Barapani and Nongpyuir. Crescentric in shape with semi circular cutting edge, this tool gradually thickens towards the butt end, which is probably meant for holding the tool while harvesting or scraping. Probably this tool must have been used as harvesters during the Neolithic. The mentioned tool is not classified in any sub-division, and hence, the 'description column' in the table would provide a better idea about the tool and its actual shape.

The Site of Umiam-Barapani (Fig. 7)

<u>Location</u>
District: Ri-Bhoi District of Meghalaya.
25⁰ 38' 55" N Latitude and 91⁰ 51' 25" E Longitude
1000-1100 M above Sea Level
Physiographic Position: Low land

Description of the Site:

The Neolithic site of *Umiam*-Barapani is located at an altitude of 1000M above sea level above the erstwhile *Umiam* River. The river flows on a much lower level alongside the site through the narrow gorges and intervening hills of the Khasi upland zone. A dam over the Umiam River was constructed in 1964 for hydro-electric power generation. Consequently, the water reservoir, commonly known as the 'Barapani Lake', covered most of the hillocks where much of the Neolithic site was located. As a result, the traces of Neolithic evidences located above the level of the lake water were recorded and probably, much of the evidences lay submerged under the lake.

The site is located at the foot of the surrounding hills that abruptly rises towards the upland zone of the southern Khasi hills plateau. From a physiographic perspective, the site is situated in a transitional belt demarcating the lowlands and undulating hills of Ri-Bhoi region on the north with the upland plateau of the East and West Khasi hills on the South.

The present floral composition of the area shows clear disparity in the pattern of vegetation which is fairly different from those of the southern upland zones. The site is located in the belt lying in transition between the sub-tropical vegetation type of the northern Ri-Bhoi region and the temperate vegetation of the southern upland zone. The disparity in the

vegetation pattern seen today may not be applied to the vegetation pattern of the prehistoric period without any paleo-botanical evidences. Although the present vegetation of Barapani and adjoining areas is characterized by pine forest, the evidence derived from the remains of tree stumps which are submerged under the lake proves that, perhaps, this area was dominated by broad leaf evergreen forest till the recent past **(Plate 2)**. A similar change in the vegetation pattern may have probably taken place throughout the southern upland zone where the primary forest was characterized by broad leaf evergreen trees. How far has human agency contributed to the destruction of the primary forest, is an interesting area of enquiry which can throw some light in understanding past-human cultural adaptation and exploitation of the environment. Although this issue is not part of the present research, yet, it is still possible to speculate that human (?) exploitation of these hills in the past have greatly reshaped the floral content of the southern upland zones that we see today (more will be discussed in a subsequent paragraph on the chapter dealing with analysis of findings).

The climatic condition in the northern low lands varies from that of the southern upland zone. The Ri-Bhoi low lands have a hot and humid summer with pleasantly warm winters. The upland zone of the Khasi and Jaintia hills experience a salubrious climate throughout the summer, but, they remain cold in the winter seasons.

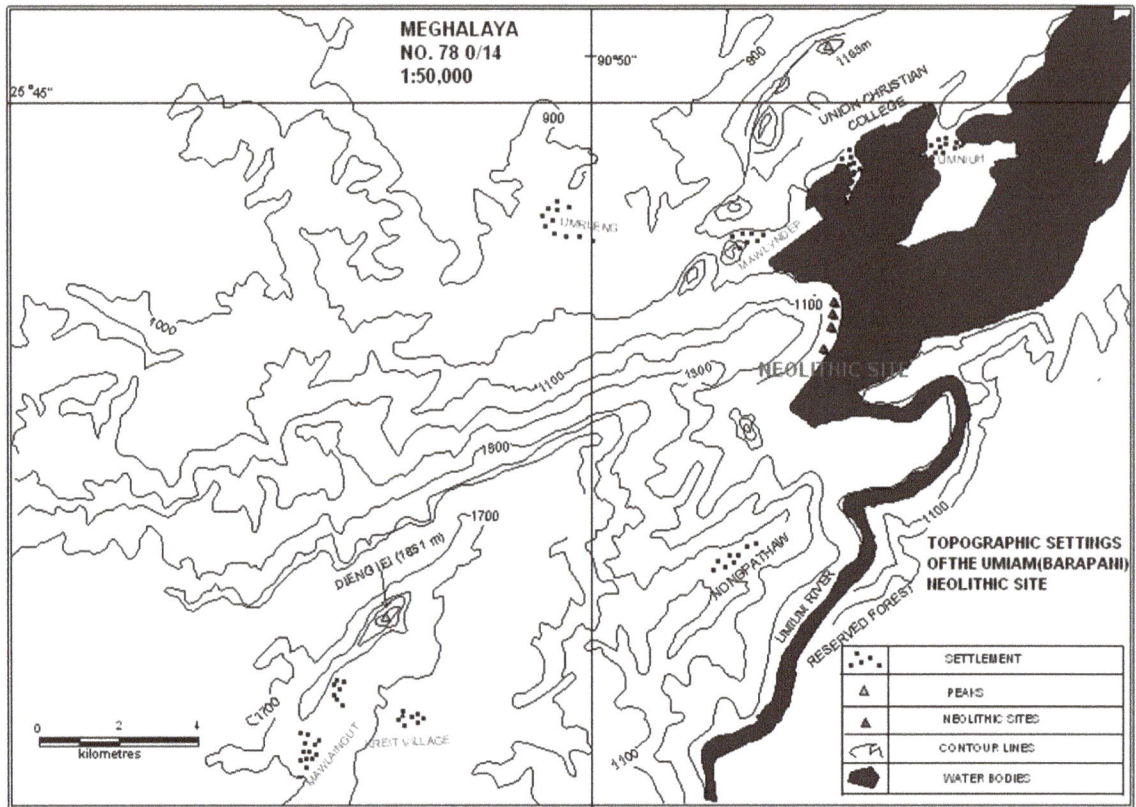

Figure 7: Topographic Settings of Umiam-Barapani Site

Climatological tables of the upland zones. Based on Observation from 1913-1960
(Sources: Simon, 1991, p. 28)

Daily Max.	Daily Min.	Highest and Date	Lowest and Date	% Relative Humidity
21ºC	12.1ºC	30.7ºC -2/5/1960	2.8ºC- 8/5/1937 & 13/2/1950	67%

The Umiam-Barapani Neolithic site is of vital importance in the context of physiographic and climatic adaption of man during the prehistoric period. This site is crucial from the archaeological perspective as it offers an interesting field study for the understanding of the micro-environmental adaptation of Neolithic man in this part of the Northeastern region.

This site of Umiam-Barapani was first reported by a team of investigators from the Anthropology department of the Gawahati University in 1979 (Hussain, 1996, pp. 111-118). Exploration of the site continued till 1995 and reports on the finds have been cited by different authors in various journals (Medhi 1990, Sharma 1991, and Bhuyan 1993)

Random surface collections of stone implements were found from the confluence of the Umiam and Umshing stream on the eastern edge of the present lake below the dam. The reported artifact assemblages from the site include axes, a shouldered celt, flakes and blade tools which are made from indurated shale (Sharma, 1991, p.51). The site has been designated as a factory site by investigators (Medhi, 1990, p.39). However, the spatial extent of the site has not been identified by the collectors.

Field surveys conducted at the site during the dry seasons when the lake water had receded to its lowest level reveal the spatial dimension of the site. This site spreads along the entire basin-like feature and the adjacent hills, as evident from the dispersal of tools which were recovered from an approximate area radius of 4Km sq **(Plate 16.B)**. Factory spots have been identified at different parts of the site away from those reported by earlier investigators. The biggest factory spot is found on the extreme western flank of the lake at the foot of *U Diengiei* hill slope, higher than the present water level of the lake and definitely much higher than the old Umiam stream[24] (Plate 16.A). The stone tool assemblages recovered from this particular spot lie in a disturbed context as there are traces of them being removed from their actual position by human agency in the process of clearing the land for the use of cultivation in the recent past. Artefacts are found scattered along the surface of the area, and quite a large number of them are artificially piled up in heaps by the farmers. All evidences, however, suggest that this area represents the largest factory spot of the site.

The tool assemblage recovered from the spot comprises of stone implements which belonged to the manufacturing stage and has been classified in this research as 'unfinished' and 'un-ground' tools. Not a single finished or ground implement was recovered from this spot. The occurrence of a large number of unfinished and unground stone implements from this single area not only explains the functional purpose of the spot but has added more information on the types and technology of tools that may be recovered later in finished form.

The stone implements collected from factory spots in and around Barapani lake include large numbers of unfinished tools occurring alongside large debris of waste flakes and cores. The contexts of these artefacts are disturbed due the impact of the lake water. During the rainy season these spots are submerged, and in the process the water erodes off the surface layer of the deposits. During the dry seasons, when the lake water recedes to the minimum, the artefacts

are found fully or partially exposed (Plate 3) on the surface and some on the layer not exceeding 15 cm below the present surface. The context of the tools is highly disturbed as they found mostly on surface of the soil which had been till by earlier cultivators. Although the cultivated mounds are already flattened by the seasonal impact of water from the lake, trace of ridges form due to the piling of dried vegetation soil and burnt to provide natural manure, are still clearly visible on the surface from where the cultural materials have been recovered. Hence, even if there is any slight trace of evidence that some tools may not have been moved from their original location, their actual depth cannot be authenticated any longer.

Most of the stone implements recovered from the different factory spots of the Umiam-Barapani site have already been worked out to their desired shape and sizes, and they can be classed as belonging to the *early stage and late-biface stage in the idealized reduction sequence* of stone tool manufacturing process. None of these stone implements are qualified to be called working or finished tools, as all them are devoid of any level of working edge (Plate 18).

There are some evidences which probably indicate that, the Neolithic people of this site have attempted to fashion tools from raw material like quartzite and carbonaceous quartzite, but they are found in very small proportion. These tools have already been worked to their desired shape but were left unfinished and without any trace of a working edge. From the receded banks of the lake, quite a number of finished tools were also recovered from the surface and a major proportion of which have been worked out of fine grain amphibolite locally called (khasi) 'green stone' and this is found as intrusive material in the Khasi and Jaintia hills. Stone implements from materials like slate and indurated shale are recovered in good numbers. Most of the stone artefacts made from amphibolite material are covered with thick layer of patina of greyish shade (Plate 23). All the finished implements are fully ground (Plate 19).

---

[24]Map No. 78 0/14 of ASSAM for United Khasi and Jaintia hills of 1910-11.
Identification of the raw material of all stone implements was made by Mr.Mansan Lyngdoh, Geologist-Directorate of Mineral Resources, Government of Meghalaya (Personal Communication).

Ring stones of various sizes which are made of indurated shale were recovered from the site **(Plate 6)**. It is interesting to note here, that all the ring stones collected were from the same spot at the top of the hillock very close to the old Umiam river.

Hand-made potsherds recovered from the site have clear cord-impressed patterns made from clay that is heavily tempered with quartz particles (Plate 7.2). These sherds are dull brown in colour, and in thickness, their measurement ranges from 0.5 cm to 0.7cm. Another category of potsherds belonging to the wheel-made variety were also collected from the site. These consisted of two globular vessels made from fine clay texture measuring between 0.2-0.4 cm in thickness (Plate 8). The manufacturing technique of these wheel-made potteries clearly suggests their association to a different cultural phase and probably to a later settlement. Taking into consideration the large number of tools that were recovered from the site, the percentage of potsherds so far discovered is extremely meager. The reason could either be; they have rolled down to the deeper level of the lake and can no longer be recovered, or they have not been used much by the people from the site[25]. One or both of these factors could be responsible for the few number of potsherds recovered from the site of Umiam-Barapani.

Clay objects of the size of a cricket ball were found from the site. But due to the impact of water they have become too loose for handling. These were probably the same types recorded from layer III from the excavation of the post-Neolithic site of Marakdola which was described by the excavator as burnt clay pellets (Rao, 1977, p.198). There is no ethnographic parallel about the use and function of these clay objects from the entire area under this present investigation.

---

[25]Ethnographic evidences shows that Bamboo is use extensively for storage purposes such as for carrying and storing water, preserving dried fishes, dry-rice bread, dried vegetables and was even used as drinking cups.

Classification of Stone Implements from the site of Umiam-Barapani.
A. <u>Finished Tools (Ground)</u>

Type	Shape	Technique	Raw Material	Maximum size in cm. LxBxT	Description
Tanged	Rectangular	Fully ground	Amphibolite	9 x 6 x 1 cm	The tenon is narrow with slight shoulders. It is slightly curved on the inner face and plano-convex; the inner face is flat while the outer face is convex. The cutting is edge beveled on the inner face.
Shouldered.	Squarish	Fully ground	Amphibolite	7 x 5 x 1 cm	The angle between the body and the tenon is close to right angle and is produced by sawing. It slightly curves and is plano-convex with the inner face flat and the outer face convex. The cutting edge bevels on the inner face.
Shouldered	Squarish	Fully ground	Slate	8.5 x 7 x 0.5 cm	Relatively thin in section. The angle between the tenon and the body is close to a right angle produced by chipping and grinding. The cutting edge is median and shows equal bifacial grinding.
Tanged	Roundish	Partially ground	Slate	8 x 7 x 0.5cm	This tool is made from a thin slate material. There is a tenon with slight trace of shoulders. Due to its almost hexagonal shape, the cutting edge median is produced by bifacial grinding and due to its use, the shape of the working edge appears rounded.
Tanged	Crescentric	Partially ground	Amphibolite	7.5 x 8.5 x 0.7cm	The tenon is seen and the shoulder slopes at an obtuse angle. The working edge is splayed and is crescentric in shape. The cutting edge is symmetrical and median which is produced through equal bifacial grinding.
Tanged	---	Partially ground	Amphibolite	8.5 x 7.5 x 1 cm	The tenon is visible and the shoulders are very shallow. Only the outer face of the tool is grounded. The cutting edge is not visible.
Tanged	Rectangular	Fully ground	Amphibolite	11 x 7.5 x 1cm	A relatively large body with small narrow tenon and weak shoulders. It is slightly curved from the section. The sides are ground flat.

Type	Shape	Technique	Raw Material	Maximum size in cm. LxBxT	Description
Shouldered.	Rectangular	Fully ground	Amphibolite	9.5 x 6.5 x.1.2cm	The tenon is comparatively big and the shoulders are almost close to right angle produced though chipping and grinding. The sides on the edge of the outer face of the body are beveled. The cutting edge is no longer visible.
Tanged	---	Fully ground	Amphibolite	6.5 x 5.5 x.1.3cm	The tenon is clearly distinguishable and the shoulders are very shallow. The cross section is lenticular and the sides are ground flat. The cutting edge median, produced through equal bifacial grinding.
Shouldered.	Rectangular	Fully ground	Shale	9 x 7 x 0.5cm	The shoulders are cut almost at a right angle and the section curves a bit on the outer face of the body. The working edge bevels on the outer face of the body and the cutting edge is produced by unequal bifacial grinding.
Tanged	Triangular	Fully ground	Amphibolite	6 x 4.3 x 1cm	The tenon is not visible but there is trace of a curve on the section of the shoulders. The sides are probably ground flat like the butt end of the tenon. The cross section is plano-convex. The beveled cutting edge is produced by unequal bifacial grinding.
Axe	Triangular	Ground	Amphibolite	7 x 6 x 0.6cm	The sides of this tool are ground flat and the cross section is slightly biconvex. The cutting edge is symmetrical and median is produced through equal bifacial grinding.
Axe	Triangular	Edge Ground ·	Amphibolite	8.5 x 6 x 0.4cm	The tool tapers towards the butt end. The section of the cutting edge is symmetrical and median produced by equal bifacial grinding. Both face of the body retain flake marks.
Axe	Triangular	Fully ground	Shale	10 x 7.5 x 0.7cm	A round butt Axe where the sides on the outer face of the body, beveled. The section is straight and the cutting edge median, produced by equal bifacial grinding.
Adze	Triangular	Fully ground	Shale	9x6x1 cm	The cross section is plano convex- flat on the inner face and beveled on both sides of the outer face. The cutting edge is beveled, produced through unequal bifacial grinding.

Type	Shape	Technique	Raw Material	Maximum size in cm. LxBxT	Description
Axe	Triangular	Fully ground	Amphibolite	8 x 6 x 1.5cm	A pointed butt axe with biconvex cross section. The sides are ground flat and the working edge is crescentric in shape. The cutting edge median, produced through equal bifacial grinding.
Adze (chisel)	Rectangular	Fully ground	Amphibolite	7 x 2.8 x 1.5cm	A bar shape which is plano in section and curved on the outer face from the center of the body to the cutting edge. The sides and the top of the butt end are ground flat. The tip of the cutting edge is broken.
Adze	Triangular	Fully ground	Amphibolite	5 x 4 x 1cm	This tool has its sides and top ground flat. The working edge beveled from the centre of the outer face of the body and the cutting edge is produced by unequal bifacial grinding.
Axe	Triangular	Fully ground	Amphibolite	6 x 3 x 1cm	This tool has a pointed butt and its sides are ground flat in shape. Both faces of the body are ground flat and the cutting edge is median, produced through bifacial grinding.
Adze	Rectangular	Fully ground	Amphibolite	8.8 x 3.2 x 2cm	Another bar shaped chisel. The sides and top are ground flat. The cutting edge beveled. Its tip is broken.
Adze	Rectangular	Natural form	Slate	-- x 6 x 0.5cm	A parallel sided celt, but broken at the butt end and hence the length cannot be measured. The cutting edge is clearly beveled. It is a long type which resembles the ones that are recorded from the sites of Umswai, Tyrso etc. near the Karbi Anglong district of Assam.
Adze	Rectangular	Fully ground	Amphibolite	8.5 x 4.3 x 1.5cm	The tool is rounded at the butt and broadens gently towards the cutting edge. The sides are ground flat. The cutting edge is broken but from a visible part it is clearly beveled.
Axe (wedge)	Triangular	Fully ground	Amphibolite	7.5 x 4.5 x 0.8cm	The sides are ground flat and the butt is slightly rounded. The section is straight. The cutting edge is symmetrical and median, produced by equal bifacial grinding.

Type	Shape	Technique	Raw Material	Maximum size in cm. LxBxT	Description
Adze (chisel)	Rectangular	Fully ground	Amphibolite	6.1 x3 x 2 cm	Another bar shape chisel with sides and top ground flat. The cross section is lenticular in shape with slight trace of convexity on the outer face of the body and beveled on the outer face of the cutting edge.
Adze (chisel)	Rectangular	Fully ground	Amphibolite	6.4 x 2.7 x 1.5 cm	Another bar shape chisel with sides and top ground flat. The cross section is lenticular in shape with slight trace of convexity on the outer face of the body. The cutting edge is not visible.
Axe (wedge?)	Triangular	Fully ground	Amphibolite	9 x 5.5 x 1.1cm	A pointed butt axe with biconvex cross section. One of the sides is ground flat while the other side is beveled from the outer face of the body. The cutting edge median is produced through equal bifacial grinding.
Not Classify	Triangular	Fully ground	Amphibolite	7 x 4 x 0.8cm	The sides are ground flat and the butt is rounded. Slightly convexity in cross section. The cutting edge is no longer visible.
Not Classify	Triangular	Fully ground	Amphibolite	10 x 5.5 x 1cm	The tool is pointed towards the butt. It is convex on the outer face and slightly concave on the inner face. The cutting edge is produced by equal bifacial grinding.
Axe	Triangular	Fully ground	Shale	8x 6x.8cm	A pointed butt axe the sides of which show slight trace of grinding. The section is straight and the cutting edge median produced by equal bi-facial grinding.
Tanged	---	Fully ground	Shale	7.8 x6.1 x.6	Highly weathered tool, straight in section with trace of median cutting edge with equal bi-facial grinding.
Axe	Triangular	Fully ground	Shale	9x5.6x – cm	This is a round butt axe with beveled and cutting edge median produced by equal bi-facial grinding. The inner face of the body is highly weathered, but there is clear indication that it is likely bi-convex.

More than 50 stone implements that are classed in this research as 'unfinished' implements were studied and analysed to get an overview on the stone tool technology in the region under-study. These tools have attained the desired shapes but they have no trace of a working edge nor are ground in any form. On the basis of their types they are categorized as follows:

A.   Quadrangular
B.   Shouldered/Tanged
C.   Pointed Butt Axe
D.   Round Butt Axe

B. Unfinished Tools (Un-ground implements)

LARGE SIZE

Type	Raw Material	Maximum size in Cm. LxBxT.
Pointed Butt	Amphibolite	14.4 x 8.7 x 2.3 cm
-do-	Amphibolite	14 x 7.4 x 1.6 cm
-do-	Slate	14.5 x 8.4 x 2 cm
-do-	Shale	16 x 10.5 x 1.5cm
Quadrangular	Amphibolite	18 x 6.5 x 0.5cm
-do-	Shale	20 x 8 x 2 cm

MEDIUM SIZE

Type	Raw Material	Maximum size in Cm. LxBxT.
Pointed Butt	Amphibolite	12 x 6 x 1.6 cm
-do-	Amphibolite	11 x 7 x 1.2cm
-do-	Amphibolite	10 x 5.5x 1 cm
Round Butt	Slate	10.4x6.2x1.5
-do-	Amphibolite	9.5 x 6 x 1 cm
-do-	Slate	12 x 7 x 1 cm
-do-	Amphibolite	11.5x5.5x1 cm
Quadrangular	Amphibolite	--x5.3x2.4 cm
-do-	Amphibolite	11x4.6x1.4
-do-	Slate	11x4.5x2cm
-do-	Amphibolite	-x4.5x1cm
-do-	Slate	10x6.5 x1.4 cm
Chisel	Slate	10x 2 x 2.5 cm
Chisel	Slate	9.3x2.9x2.7cm
Chisel	Slate	9.8x3.3x2.3cm
Shouldered	Amphibolite	12.5x7.5x2.5 cm
-do-	Amphibolite	9.2x6x1.3cm
Tanged	Amphibolite	9.5 x 6 x 1.3cm

SMALL SIZE

Type	Raw Material	Maximum size in Cm. LxBxT.
Pointed Butt	Amphibolite	9.3 x 6.2 x 1.3cm
-do-	Amphibolite	9.2 x 4.6 x 1 cm
-do-	Amphibolite	9.4x5.8x 1.3cm
-do-	Amphibolite	9.9x5.2x1.1 cm
-do-	Amphibolite	8.1x5x1.2cm
-do-	Amphibolite	7.5x5.1x 0.7cm
-do-	Amphibolite	9.2.x4.9x1.2cm
-do-	Amphibolite	7.7x 4.4x1.2cm
-do-	Amphibolite	8.7x 5.3x1.2cm

-do-	Amphibolite	9.4x 5.2x1.3cm
-do-	Amphibolite	8x5x1.6cm
-do-	Amphibolite	8.6x 5.9x.9cm
-do-	Slate	8.7x5.6x0.4cm
Round Butt	Amphibolite	8.1x 4.6x.1.3 cm
-do-	Amphibolite	7.4x5.2x1.4cm
-do-	Amphibolite	8x 5.9x1.6cm

C. Ring Stones

Maximum Thickness	Diameter of the centre hole.	Diameter of outer Ring
2 cm	1.8 cm	11.6 cm
--	3.6 cm	12.8 cm
2.3 cm	1.4 cm	11.7 cm
1.4 cm	1.8 cm	10 cm
1.5 cm	1.9 cm	13.5 cm
0.7 cm	1.5 cm	5.7 cm
--	2.7 cm	8.2 cm
2.2 cm	2.2 cm	11.8 cm
--	--	7.2 cm

Ceramic evidences from Umiam-Barapani (Plate 7.2)

As already mentioned very few ceramic evidences have been recovered from the site. Only three pieces of hand-made potteries were recovered, and one rim-piece of what appears to be a carinated pot can be distinguished. The ceramic materials from the site were burnt at a very low temperature as seen from the bigger space of the dark core at the section profile of the sherds. They are of dull brown colour and one of the pieces retained the black tinge due to the direct firing technique. There are clear traces of quartz grits on the outer surface of the sherds. Except for the rimed sherd, the other two pottery pieces bear cord-impressed patterns in the form of horizontal lines on the outer surface, probably because of the beater and pad method, a characteristic feature of the potting technology in the region (Sharma, 1967, pp.126-128). Two pieces of partially intact pottery were also found made of fine wheel clay and having a globular shape. This probably belonging to a more recent period, since, settlement in the area continued till the 1950's before the hydro electric dam project displaced the population from the area.

44

The Site of Sohpet-Bneng Hill (Fig. 8)

<u>Location</u>
District: Ri-Bhoi District of Meghalaya
25⁰ 42' 26" N Latitude and 91⁰ 55' 40" E Longitude
1200-1300 M above Sea Level
Physiographic Position: Low land

This Neolithic site lies about 4 kilometers aerially, north-east of the Umiam-Barapani site at an altitude of 1200 M above Sea level. It is located on the *Sohpet Bneng* hill, translated as the Navel String of Heaven, and lies close to a small village called Law Nongthroh[26]. Situated at a higher elevation it gives a bird's eye view of the entire Umiam-Barapani site. The vegetation of the area is characterized by pine trees with patches of evergreen forest. Local Khasi tradition claimed that the hill was the ancestral home of the entire Khasi race[27]. The folk story associated with the hill which made clear reference about the presence of human settlement on the hill provided useful information which can add additional support to the archaeological finding from this site.

Neolithic stone implements in association with ceramic potsherds were collected from a tilled jhum field at the top of one of the hillocks. Altogether, thirteen finished-(used) stone implements were recovered from the site, twelve of which were recovered from an area within 100 square meters and in association with potsherds. A single implement was found about a kilometer away from the rest, and this has added more information about the spatial extent of the site.

Apart from the Neolithic implements, other cultural materials which belonged to a different cultural phase were also recorded at the site. These include fine wheel-made potteries and iron slag[28], large number of Megalithic monuments comprising of menhir-dolmens and burial cist monuments, spread around the site. Seven cremation platforms are also found in this area close to the place from where the Neolithic implements were collected. The historical context of these Megalithic monuments and the platforms is still preserved in the oral tradition of the local people who associate them to a settlement which later on became headquarter of a province in the past[29]. The old settlement was also located at the lower ridge where wheel-made potteries have been recovered.

---

[26]This village came into existence only a few decades back and is populated by people who came to farm in these hills from other parts of the khasi hills. Oral tradition claim that in the past, the people spent a night at this place to prepare for the major religious ceremony which would take place on the following day at the apex of the Sohpet Bneng Peak. They perform dance and egg-breaking ritual. The sacrificial Ram was prepared and adorned at this place.

[27]The Folk stories associated with the hill already discussed in the preceeding chapter.

[28]A chunk of Iron slag was found within close proximity to the Neolithic site, probably an ancient smelting place.

[29]The main informant is the *Basan* or an Elder (Mr. Everest Rangslang) of the Mawbuh Province at Umroi village, who claimed that his clan is directly descended from the people that initiated the first religious ceremony at the apex of U Sohpet Bneng hill and who inhabited this same area where the Neolithic and Megalithic evidences are recorded.

Classification of Neolithic Stone Implements from Sohpet Bneng Site (Plate 4)

<u>Finished Tools</u>: Ground

Shape	Type	Raw Material	Maximum size in Cm. LxBxT.	Description
Squarish	Shouldered	Slate	7 x 6.5 x 0.7 cm	The shoulders are cut almost at right angles through the process of sawing. The sides are ground flat. The tenon is square in shape and prominent in size. The cutting edge shows signs of secondary grinding and the tip of the working edge is no longer visible.
Almost squarish	Shouldered	Amphibolite	5.5 x5x 0.5 cm	The shoulders are produced by sawing. The body tapers towards the butt end and sides are ground flat. The cutting is symmetrical and median through equal bifacial grinding.
Round	Shouldered	Slate	5.4 x 6.2 x 0.3 cm	This tool is made from a very thin slate. It has shallow and sloping shoulders produced by chipping and grinding. The cutting edge is symmetrical and median, produced through bifacial grinding. Due to its uses, the shape of the cutting edge is almost crescentric.
Squarish	Shouldered	Amphibolite	7.4 x 6.3 x 0.7 cm	The shoulders are formed at an acute angle. The cross section is bi-convex and the sides and butt end of the tenon are ground flat. The cutting edge is symmetrical and median, produced through equal bifacial grinding.
Rectangular	Adze (Chisel)	Amphibolite	6.8 x 3.3 x 1.8 cm	A bar shape, chisel with parallel sides. The butt end is ground flat. The cross section is lenticular in shape. The cutting edge on the outer face beveled, and the working edge is splayed.
Rectangular	Adze (Chisel)	Slate	6.4 x1.8 x 1.5 cm	A parallel bar shape chisel with sides and the top ground flat. The cutting edge on the outer face beveled. The tip of the working edge is no longer visible.
Rectangular	Adze (Chisel)	Shale	8 x 3.2 x 1.7 cm	This is a bar shape chisel having parallel sides. The top is ground flat. The cutting edge median, produced though equal bifacial grinding. Through use, the tool is highly weathered with large traces of used marks are seen.
Rectangular	Adze	Amphibolite	6 x 4 x 1 cm	The butt tool is rounded and the sides are ground flat. The cross section is plano-convex and the cutting edge is beveled.
Triangular	Axe (wedge)	Shale	7 x 5.7 x 0.6 cm	An axe with broad cutting edge straight in section and the sides and top are ground flat. It narrows towards the butt end. The cutting edge is symmetrical and median, produced by equal bifacial grinding.
----	Axe ?	Amphibolite	-- x 6 x 0.7	The butt end of the tool is broken but there is an indication that it narrows down towards the butt. The sides are ground flat. The cutting edge median, produced by equal bifacial grinding.

Shape	Type	Raw Material	Maximum size in Cm. LxBxT.	Description
Triangular	Axe	Amphibolite	7.4 x 5.5 x 2.2 cm	A round butt type of axe and the edge of the sides is beveled. The cross section is biconvex. The tool showed traces of use-marks along its surface. The cutting edge is no longer visible.
---	Not Classify	Amphibolite	9.2 x 5.2 x 1.9 cm	An unfinished tool. It has a pointed butt. The tool bears flake scars on both faces of the body.

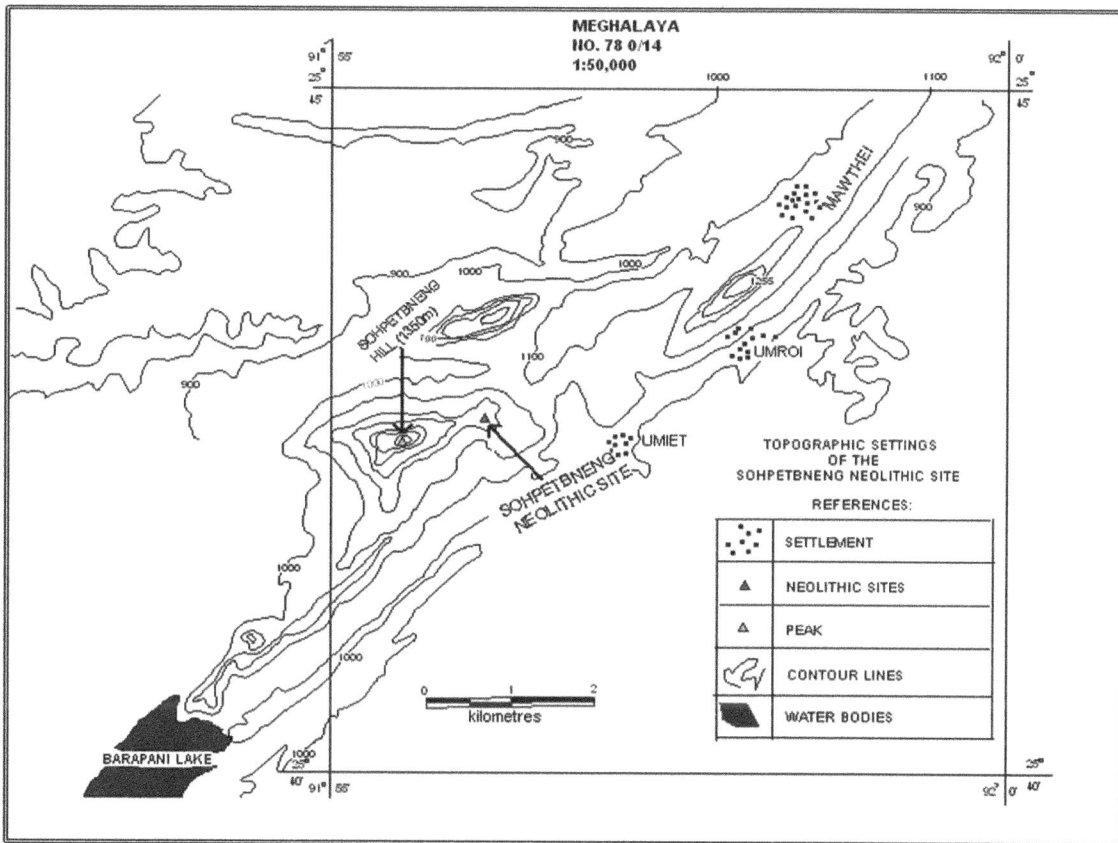

Figure 8: Topographic Settings of Sohpet-Bneng Site

Ceramic evidences from Sohpet Bneng Site (Plate 7.1)

More than 26 numbers of potsherd pieces were recovered from the spot where the maximum numbers of Neolithic stone tools were found. The pottery ware of the site are of two varieties; the coarse hand-made and the fine-slipped wheel made variety. The differences in the manufacturing technique of the two types of potsherds, clearly pointed to their separate cultural association and this is apparent even without stratigraphic evidences, considering the fact that the area was continuously occupied to a much latter period as evident from the megalithic monuments and the funeral platforms as indeed oral traditions. The hand-made varieties were fired at a very low temperature as evident from the bigger space of the dark core at the section profile of the potsherds. They are dull chocolate-brown in colour, devoid of any form of slip. They are made from very coarse quality clay

47

with heavily tempered quartz particles which is prominently visible on the outer surface of all the sherds from this category. In thickness, they measure a maximum of 0.9cm and a minimum of 0.3cm. All the hand-made potsherds in the collection bear two types of cord-impressed patterns on their outer surface. The finer ones with comparatively thin-section and dull-chocolate in colour, bears twisted cord impressed pattern, while the thicker ones and coarser variety with dull-brown colour, bears a prominent horizontal cord impressed pattern. Like the sherd pieces from Umiam-Barapani, these patterns were produced due to the beater and pad method technique a characteristic feature of the potting technology of the region.

The Site of Mawrong (See Fig. 12 for Reference)

<u>Location</u>
District: Ri-Bhoi District of Meghalaya
$25^0 51'$ --" N Latitude and $91^0 59'$--" E Longitude
900-1000 M Above Sea Level
Physiographic Position: Low land

The site of Mawrong from where Neolithic stone tools were recovered is located close to the Mawrong village about 16 Km from Umsning township on the National Highway[30]. The Umran stream runs very close on the eastern fringe of the village. The flora of the area is identified with sub-tropical vegetation and the climate is hot and humid. Besides the paddy field cultivation, shifting or jhum continues to be the dominant method of cultivation for certain crops of the people of the village.

Neolithic stone implements were collected from the surface along the eastern foothill of the hillock where the present village is situated, ranging at an altitude of 800-900 meters above sea level. These tools were found mostly from the terrace surface of the hill and they have been unearthed when the land was tilled for jhum cultivation. The entire collections of stone implements from this village were found from separate locations occurring at an interval of roughly 20 meters from each other. The local people of the village, especially the cultivators have reported the findings of such Neolithic stone tools from almost all directions within and around the periphery of the village from jhum fields. All the stone implements from this site are of the finished stage.

Classification of Stone Implements from the site of Mawrong (Plate 4)

<u>Finished Tools</u>: Ground

Shape	Type	Raw Material	Maximum size in Cm. LxBxT.	Description
Squarish	Shouldered	Slate	6.6x 6.2 x 0.5 cm	The shoulders are cut near to right angles, produced by sawing. The sides are ground flat and the tenon is square in shape. The cutting edge symmetrical and median produced by equal bifacial grinding.
Squarish	Shouldered	Slate	6.8 x 6 x 0.5 cm	The shoulders of the tool are cut almost at right angles produced by sawing. The tenon is square in shape. The cutting edge showed signs of secondary grinding and re-use. The sides are ground flat and the cutting edge is blunt and no longer visible.
Squarish	Shouldered	Slate	7.1 x 6.6 x 0.5 cm	A flat tool whose shoulders are sawn at right angles. The sides are ground flat and the tenon is square in shape. The cutting edge is symmetrical and median, produced by equal bifacial grinding.
Almost squarish	Shouldered	Slate	7.6 x 7.2 x 0.5 cm	The shoulders are almost at right angles and were produced by sawing. The tenon is square in shape. The sides and the top of the tenon are ground flat. The cutting edge symmetrical and median, produced by equal bifacial grinding.

---

[30]It is located on the side of the National Highway No. 40 about 33 Kms from Shillong.

49

Shape	Type	Raw Material	Maximum size in Cm. LxBxT.	Description
Almost squarish	Shouldered	Amphibolite	5.4 x 4.6 x 1.2 cm	A small specimen of a shouldered tool and relatively thick in cross-section. The shoulders obtuse, but neatly sawn. The sides and butt end of the tenon are ground flat and cutting edge median, produced by equal bifacial grinding.
Triangular	Axe (wedge)	Amphibolite	8.5 x 5.9 x 1 cm	The sides and butt end are ground flat. The cross section is slightly bi-convex. The cutting edge is symmetrical and median, produced by equal bifacial grinding.
Triangular	Axe (wedge)	Slate	8 x 5.5 x 0.5 cm	A flat pointed butt axe with sides, ground flat. The cutting edge is symmetrical and median, produced by equal bifacial grinding. The working edge is crescentric in shape,
Triangular	Adze	Amphibolite	9 x 6.2 x 1 cm	A tool tapers towards the butt end which is almost pointed. The cross section bi-convex and beveled on both faces of the edges on the sides of the body. Only one face of the cutting edge is grounded, produced by unequal bifacial grinding. The tip of the cutting edge is broken.
Triangular	Axe	Slate	10.2 x 6.4 x 1.2 cm	This is a round butt axe beveled on the edge of the sides of the outer face and rounded to the butt end. The tool is highly weathered and the cutting edge is no longer visible.
Almost Rectangular	Axe	Amphibolite	7 x 3.9 x 1.2 cm	Probably rounded on the butt end. The sides are ground flat and section lenticular in shape and bi-convex. The cutting edge is symmetrical and median produced by equal bifacial grinding
Triangular	Axe (Splayed)	Sandstone	4.8 x 4.9 x 1 cm	A small specimen of splayed axe. The sides are ground flat and the section, lenticular in shape and bi-convex. The cutting edge median, produced by equal bifacial grinding.
Almost Rectangular	Axe (wedge)	Sandstone	6.4 x 4 x 0.5 cm	A small round butt axe whose sides are ground flat. It is thin in section and slightly bi-convex. The cutting edge symmetrical and is produced by equal bifacial grinding.
Rectangular	Axe	Slate	-x 6 x 1cm	Only half part of the tool is intact. It is probably a pointed-butt axe beveled on either side of the edge of the body. The section bi-convex and the cutting median produced by equal bifacial grinding.

The Site of Mawbri (See Fig.12 for Reference)

<u>Location</u>
District: Ri-Bhoi District of Meghalaya
900-1000 M Above Sea Level
Physiographic Position: Low land

The village of Mawbri is located south of Mawrong village on the road leading to Karbi Anglong district of Assam. The Umtung stream which joins the Umkhen river on the north, flows through the village. Shifting or jhum method continues to be a dominant form of agricultural practice of the people of the village till today.

The Neolithic stone implements from the site have been collected from the surface of various jhum fields located close to the settlement area of the village. The local people of the village frequently reported finding Neolithic implements which is locally known as *Sdie pyrthat* or thunder axe from their jhum fields especially those that are located along the slopes of the foothills. The area shows great potential for further investigation.

Classification of Stone Implements Mawbri Site (Plate 9)

<u>Finished Tools:</u> Ground

Shape	Type	Raw Material	Maximum size in Cm. LxBxT.	Description
Triangular	Axe	Slate	9 x 5.6 x 1	A flat round-butt axe. The edge of the outer face of the body beveled, and the cutting is no longer visible.
Triangular	Axe (wedge)	Amphibolite	7.4x5.5x2	A tool with pointed butt and broader towards the cutting edge. The sides and the butt end are ground flat. The cutting edge median produced through equal bifacial grinding.
Rectangular	Shouldered (Spear head)	Shale	17 x 5.5 x 1	The tool is flat and relatively long. The tenon is very small and narrow. It is beveled on the edge of both sides of the inner and outer faces. The sides are ground. The body of the tool tapers towards the cutting edge. Although one part of the tip is not visible, its projection is definitely pointed. The tool has the shape of a lance or spear-head.

Shape	Type	Raw Material	Maximum size in Cm. LxBxT.	Description
Rectangular	Shouldered	Amphibolite	16 x 6 x 2	The tool is relatively large compared with the rest in the collection. The tenon is small compared to the size of the body and the shoulders are cut at right angles. Metal must have been used for sawing the shoulders which was cut at perfect right angles. The entire body of the tool is highly polished having a glazed surface. From the section profile of the tool, it is slightly concave on the inner face and at the cutting edge. The tool tapers towards the butt end. The sides and butt end of the tenon are ground flat. The working edge beveled produced through unifacial grinding. This tool was probably meant for carpentry use perhaps for chiseling hard wood[31]
Almost Squarish	Shouldered	Shale	8x5.5x.6	The shoulders are cut almost at right angles and they are produced through sawing. The tenon is square in shape. The sides and butt end of the tenon are ground flat and the section convex-sided. The cutting edge symmetrical and median, produced by equal bifacial grinding.
Rectangular?	Adze	Slate	--x8x.7	A flat celt with only the cutting edge portion of the tool being visible. Since the butt part of the body is broken, therefore the length cannot be measured. The sides are ground flat and the cutting edge beveled, through unifacial grinding.
Triangular	Axe (wedge)	Amphibolite	7x5x1.2	A pointed-butt axe which tapers towards the butt end. The sides are ground flat and the section bi-convex. The cutting edge median, produced by equal bifacial grinding.
Triangular	Axe	Amphibolite	11.6x5.6x2	A pointed butt Axe and section bi-convex. The cutting edge appears to be median. The sides are rounded. The tool shows trace of being used and much of its body is weathered.
Triangular	Axe	Shale	8x4.6x0.7	A pointed-butt Axe having plano-convex section; flat in the inner face and convex on the outer face. The edges of the outer face of the body beveled. The edge is also beveled. The tool is partially broken at the working edge.

---

[31]This resembles the Regular and Long type of Variety E.II of tool recorded in Dani's collection. These types are not known in Assam but have been found in southern Burma. See A.H. Dani. *Pre and Proto-History of Eastern India*, 1960 Calcutta, p. 82.

The Site of Iapngar (See Fig. 12 for Reference)

<u>Location</u>
District: Ri-Bhoi District of Meghalaya
900-1000 m Above Sea Level
Physiographic Position: Low land

This site lies east of the site of Mawbri and close to Karbi Anglong district of Assam. The Umtung stream flows close to the village and the present settlement is at the foot of the hill. An older settlement[32] was discovered at the top of the hill where a large number of cist burials and megalithic monuments like menhirs and dolmens are found along with large numbers of potsherds. Jhum cultivation is the primary method of agriculture adopted by the people of this area today.

All the tools from the site were collected from the surface of various jhum fields especially from the hill slopes. Ethnographic survey of the village and the surrounding areas of the site show an admixture of two communities occupying the area, namely, the Khasi-Bhoi community and the Karbi community also known as the Mikirs, living side by side. Intermarriage between the two communities is common. Both communities are well acquainted with the concept of 'Thunder Axe'[33] and they have their own term for it. The local people report of their constant encounter with varieties of Neolithic tools from their Jhum fields[34].

Classification of Stone Implements from the site of Iapngar (Plate 10)
<u>Finished Tools:</u> Ground

Shape	Type	Raw Material	Maximum size in Cm. LxBxT.	Description
Almost squarish	Tanged	Shale	6.5 x5.2 x.9	The tenon very prominent and shoulders are shallow produced through sawing. The tool tapers gently towards the tenon. The sides are ground flat and the cutting edge median.
Almost squarish	Shouldered	Slate	7.2 x5.5 x.5	Well-cutted shoulders is seen on the tool. The sides are ground flat and the cutting edge median.
Triangular	Axe	Slate	5.9 x5.5 x.3	The tool tapers towards the butt end which is pointed. The sides are ground flat and the cutting edge median, produced through equal bifacial grinding.

---

[32]The local villagers claimed that this site was their previous village. The presence of a large amount of potsherds, megalithic cist burials, standing megalithic monuments and foot paths certainly prove the existence of a settlement in the past. A trence of 4ft wide and and 6ft deep more or less, was dug all along the boundary of the settlement which was used as a moat (without water) for the defence of the village.

[33]See the chapter 3 on 'Ethnoarcheology' dealing with the concept of Thunder Axe.

[34] The Karbi people are more acquainted with the Thunder Axe than the Khasis of the uplands. It may be noted that Jhum cultivation is practice more commonly by the Karbi tribe than the Khasis.

Shape	Type	Raw Material	Maximum size in Cm. LxBxT.	Description
Triangular	Adze	Sandstone	7.9 x5.5 x 2.8	The tool has a pointed butt, plano-convex in section; flat on one face and curved from the cutting edge to the butt. It is thick in section.
Rectangular	Axe	Shale	5.8 x4.2 x.7	A facetted tool, almost parallel sided with a rounded butt. The sides are ground flat and the section lenticular in shape. The cutting edge median, produced by bifacial grinding.
Triangular	Axe	Slate	- x6 x1	The butt end is broken but it definitely tapers towards the butt end. The cross section is bi-convex and sides grounded. The cutting edge median produce through equal bifacial grinding.
Triangular	Adze	Slate	10.5 x6 x1	A round butt tool with sides beveled. The section is plano-convex, flat on one face ad curved from the cutting edge to the butt. The cutting edge unifacial.
Rectangular	Axe	Slate	9.5 x6.3 x 1.3	This is a rounded butt tool. The tool is highly weathered on both faces of the body.
Likely Rectangular	Not Classify	Slate	- x8.3 x.9	The tool is broken but the projection from what is left shows clearly that this is a parallel sided rectangular celt. The side which is visible shows that it is ground flat. The cutting edge median, produce through equal bifacial grinding.

The Sites of Tyrso, Umswai, Amjong, and Umbi
<u>Location</u>
District: Ri-Bhoi District of Meghalaya
900-1000 M Above Sea Level
Physiographic Position: Low land

The tools from this area were recovered from four different villages, namely, Umbi, Umswai, Amjong including Tyrso. All these villages are located on the extreme northern border of the Khasi and Jaintia hills very close to the Karbi Anglong district of Assam. The vegetation type is sub-tropical identified with broad leaf forest while the climate is hot and humid. These villages reveal great admixture of Karbi or Mikir communities living in very close association with the Khasi-Bhoi population. The areas around these parts are densely vegetated and jhum cultivation is still the dominant agricultural practice. Local people of these areas also claim of their frequent encounter with Neolithic implements while clearing the land for jhum cultivation. The area is highly significant from an archaeological point of view, because firstly, the present ethnographic composition of the villages proves that this was the meeting place of two major communities of North east India, namely, the Karbi-Mirkir tribe and the Bhoi and Jaintia communities of the Khasi tribe in the past and hence can help to provide important answers to the movement pattern of the population into the Khasi and Jaintia hills right from the Neolithic period onwards. Secondly, the area also lies in the transitional belt of the lower Brahmaputra valley and the Khasi plateau and such a geographical position may throw some information about the adaptation pattern and adaption process of the Neolithic folk. The presence of a large number of Megalithic monuments around the area, especially at Umswai adds another significant aspect to the importance of the area from the context of understanding the cultural transition between the Neolithic-Megalithic phase in this part of North East India.

Classification of Stone Implements from the sites of Tyrso, Umswai, Amjong, and Umbi. (Plate 14)

<u>Finished Tools: Ground</u>

Type	Shape	Raw Material	Maximum size in Cm. LxBxT.	Description
Adze	Triangular	Shale	12 x 6.4 x 1.5	A flat celt, beveled at the working edge. The sides are ground flat. The butt end of the tool is broken.
Axe	Rectangular	Shale	9.5 x 6 x 1	Another flat celt with equal bifacial grinding at the cutting edge
Adze	Rectangular	Shale	10.2 x 5.8 x 1	Flat celt and beveled at the working edge. The sides are ground flat. The butt end of the tool is broken.
Adze	Rectangular	Pebble	9.8 x 5.3 x 1.5	Bi-convex with equal bifacial grinding. The sides ground flat. The raw material used is different from rest in the assemblage.
Adze	Rectangular	Shale	12.8 x 3.5 x 1.1	A parallel sided longish-celt and the working edge beveled. The side profile is plano-convex and beveled on the section. The butt end is ground flat and its function is more like a chisel.
Adze	Rectangular	Shale	13.1 x 7 x 1.4	A flat celt beveled at the working edge. The sides are ground flat and the butt end of the tool is broken. The tool tapers slightly towards the butt end

The Site of Nongkhrah (See Fig. 12 for Reference)

<u>Location</u>
District: Ri-Bhoi District of Meghalaya
800-900 m Above Sea Level
Physiographic Position: Low land

The site of Nongkhrah lies close to the township of Nongpoh on the National Highway between the towns of Shillong and Gawahati. Jhum is the primary method of cultivation adopted by the people of the village. Only a single stone tool was collected from the surface of a jhum field from this site. Local people claim that such stone implements are often encountered by them during the clearance of their jhum fields. The site also shows evidence of stone cists which contain post-cremated bones.

Classification of Stone Implements from the site of Nongkhrah (Plate 14)

<u>Finished Tools</u>: Ground

Shape	Type	Raw Material	Maximum size in Cm. LxBxT.	Description
Rectangular	Adze	Amphibolite	9.2x4.5x2.2	An unusual type in the entire collection from the region. The tool has a rounded butt with lenticular cross section and the side profile plano-convex. It has semi-circular notches at both sides produced by grinding. The cutting edge beveled. The notches were meant for hafting the tool like an adze[35].

---

[35]This resembles the Class A:-Facetted Tool of Variety A.IV recorded by Dani from Naga hills in A.H. Dani. *Pre and Proto-History of Eastern India*, 1960 Calcutta, p. 63.

The Site of Umjajew (Fig. 9)

<u>Location</u>
District: East Khasi Hills District. Meghalaya
91⁰51'50" East Longitude and 25⁰36'10"North Latitude
1200-1300 M above Sea level
Physiographic Position: Upland

The site of Umjajew (Arrow Mark Plate 16.A) is a direct extension the Umiam-Barapani Neolithic site lying south and overlooking the latter from a higher altitude. The site is located at the edge of the upland zone which in the context of this research is the point that separates the Khasi upland of the central Meghalaya plateau and the Ri-Bhoi lowlands of the north. East of this site and below the steep gorge runs the Umiam stream which flows along the channel that separates two intervening hills of the east and the west Khasi hills. The site overlooks the entire course of the Umiam stream as it flows towards the Ri-Bhoi lowlands along its northern course. Neolithic finds from the site include some finished stone implements, but the major composition of this site is debris of large amount of waste flakes and cores found scattered throughout the site. This was probably a factory site and the evidence of finished tools, suggest that it was also occupied by the Neolithic people as a settlement also. All the characteristic feature of the site seems to show its direct link with the adjoining Umiam-Barapani site. Trace of a secondary iron smelting spot was found at the site and Iron slag was also recovered in large quantities.

Classification of Stone Implements from the site of Umjajew (Plate 11)

<u>Finished Tools: Ground</u>

Shape	Type	Raw Material	Maximum size in Cm. LxBxT.	Description
Oval	Tanged	Amphibolite	9 x 7.8 x 1.1	The shoulders are barely visible and tenon is relatively very small. The section profile bi-convex. The cutting edge median, produced through equal bifacial grinding The tool splayed towards the working edge which is crescentric in shape.
Triangular	Axe	Amphibolite	7.2 x 4 x 2	Wedge-Axe with broad cutting edge that tapers towards the butt end. It has a thick cross section. The sides are ground flat. The cutting edge splayed and median, produced through equal bifacial grinding. Due to its use, the front part of the cutting edge of the tool is partially broken.
Rectangular	Adze (Chisel)	Amphibolite	8.8 x 1.9 x 2	A bar shaped tool with parallel sides. It is a chisel but with equal bifacial grinding at the cutting edge. The cross section is lenticular in shape and only the working edge has been ground. Both faces of the tool retains flake scars.

Unfinished Tools:

Plate No. 5

Unfinished tools are found in large numbers at this site but only the few below were chosen for analysis in order to understand the nature of the industry.

Shape	Type	Raw Material	Maximum size in Cm. LxBxT.	Description
Triangular	Medium	Amphibolite	10.8x9.7x1.4	Oval shape like axe with broad cutting edge. The tool is probably in the manufacturing stage and unfinished. The entire tool bears flake scars without any trace of grinding.
Shouldered	Medium	Amphibolite	12 x7x 1	A shouldered tool which was left unfinished. The tool shows no trace of grinding.
Rectangular	Medium	Amphibolite	9x3.3 x 2.6	A parallel sided chisel in an unfinished stage. The cutting edge has been flaked and slanted from the middle of the body on the outer face while the inner face is left flat. There is no trace of grinding.

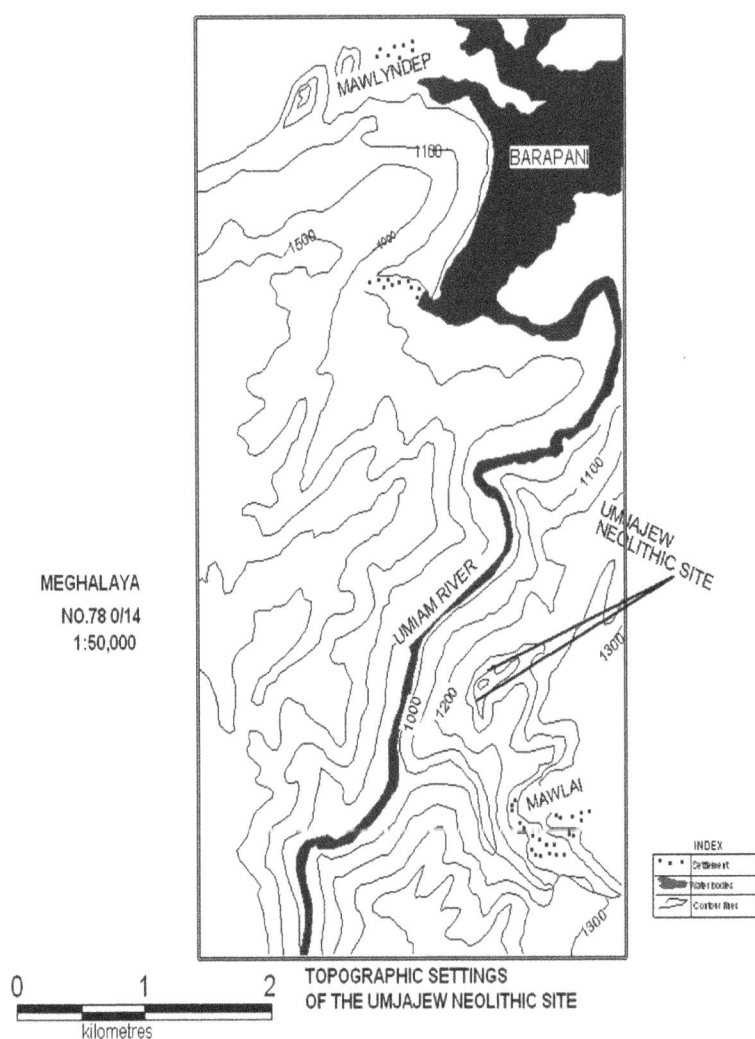

Figure 9: Topographic Settings of Umjajew Site

58

The Site of Upper Shillong San-Mer (Fig. 10)

Location
91°51'15" East Longitude and 25°32'40" North Latitude
1600-1700 m Above Sea Level
District: East Khasi Hills District. Meghalaya
Physiographic Position: Upland

The site of Upper Shillong (San Mer) is located further south of the Umjajew site and like the former site to its west approximately 2 kilometers below the steep gorge runs the Umiam stream which flows along the channel that separates two intervening hills, of the east and the west Khasi hills. This is an extensive site spreading over a large area. Field investigation was conducted on three areas of the site where the evidence of cultural materials are more concentrated. All the three areas of the site definitely belong to the same cultural level. The only material used for stone implements is amphibolite which is easily available in close proximity.

The first part of the site is located at the reserved forest area on the eastern side of the road that leads to Cherrapunji from Shillong. From this part of the site, only a single piece of finished stone implement was recovered during the digging of a drain for water pipeline. Large amount of waste flakes and unfinished Neolithic tools were however found throughout the site within 10 cm from the surface. Random digging of the site showed that these unfinished tools were already disturbed located at a depth of 10-30cm below the present surface which is immediately followed by layer of compact soil. The texture of the soil from where the cultural material was found is very loose with signs of burning showing regular jhumming agricultural activity taking place in the area in the past. Potsherds of handmade variety were also recovered from the site (Pate 7.3), and they were found alongside with the waste flakes and unfinished tools.

The second part of the site lies west of the present Shillong-Cherrapunji road and opposite the above site. Debris of stone materials in the form of waste flakes and cores were found underneath a layer where rows of Megalithic monuments stand erected (Plate 13). The Neolithic stone evidences in this area were at the depth of 10-20 cm, below the present[36] megalithic surface. The presence of these Megalithic monument provided additional insights into the transition of Neolithic to Megalithic cultural phase in these hills especially in the context of understanding the intra-hills migration and the beginning of social formation.

The third part of the site lies about a kilometer further south along the same direction of the above mentioned site. The waste flakes and cores from this area is spread over a very wide area and comparatively denser in concentration than the above two areas. A trial digging of this part of the site reveals the concentration of cultural materials which starts right from the surface and in some patches continues undisturbed to almost 3 feet below the surface (Plate 13). The soil where these cultural materials were found is similar to the above mentioned site, which is loose in texture with evidence of burning. Although this site was certainly used by cultivators in the past, the recurring evidence and density in the concentration of cultural material does not however seem to indicate that they have been piled up artificially but nonetheless, are secondary in context. This area was probably used as dumping ground for discarded stone debris or was a stone making industry for quite a long period of time.

---

[36]The same space was used as a factory site and was probably later, choosen as the space for erecting Megalithic monuments.

Classification of Stone Implements from the site of Upper Shillong (San Mer) (Plate 11)

Finished Tools: Ground Tools

Shape	Type	Raw Material	Maximum size in Cm. LxBxT.	Description
Rectangular	Adze	Amphibolite	6 x 4 x 1 cm	A curvilinear type with lenticular cross section and convex-sided. The sides are ground flat and the butt of the tool is rounded. The cutting edge beveled.

Unfinished Tools

A large number of unfinished tools were also recovered from this site. In fact this is a factory site with a large number of waste flakes and core tools which were discarded and left unfinished. All the unfinished stone implements from this site are made of amphibolite with thick tinge of patina on the surface. No classification was made of the tools as they resemble the same type from the unfinished varieties found at Umiam-Barapani and Umjajew sites.

Ceramic evidences from Upper-Shillong (San Mer) (Plate 7.3)

More than 25 numbers of potsherds were recovered from the spot where the maximum Neolithic stone tools were found. The hand-made varieties were fired at a very low temperature as evident from the bigger space of the dark core at the section profile of the potsherds. They are dull brown in colour, without any slip. They are made from very coarse quality amphibolite with heavily tempered quartz particles which is prominently visible on the outer surface of all the sherds from this category. In thickness, they measure a maximum of 0.11 cm and a minimum of 0.5 cm. All the hand-made potsherds in the collection bear distinct horizontal cord-impressed patterns on their outer surface with incised marks at the rim part. Like the sherd pieces from Umiam-Barapani, and Sohpet Bneng sites, these patterns were produced due to the beater and pad method technique a characteristic feature of the potting technology of the region.

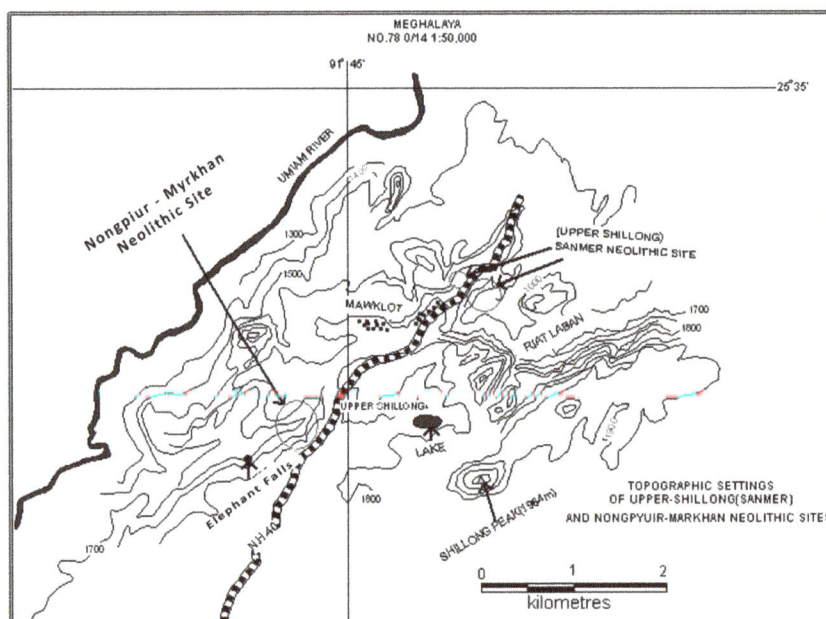

Figure 10: Topographic Settings of Upper-Shillong (San-Mer) Site

The Site of Nongpyiur-Myrkhan (See Fig. 12 for Reference)

<u>Location</u>
District: East Khasi Hills District. Meghalaya
91°49′32″ East Longitude and 25°32′30″ North Latitude
1600-1700 m above Sea Level.
Physiographic Position: Upland

This site has been named after two separate villages located close to each other. The site of Nongpyiur lies about 2.5 kilometers east of the Umiam stream and it is located close to the *elephants* falls which flows from the Shillong Peak hills and flows westwards to join the Umiam stream. The site of Myrkhan lies below Nongpyiur and just above the eastern gorge of the Umiam stream. The stone implements recovered from the site, clearly proves that this site is an extension of the Umiam-Barapani, Umjajew and Upper-Shillong (San-Mer) Neolithic site. The local people of these villages are very familiar with the Neolithic tools and they also claim to have found lots of finished stone objects while cultivating their fields. The site has great potential for an in-depth study on the Neolithic culture.

At the site of Nongpyiur, large numbers of Neolithic waste stone flakes were found across the area, close to a small stream. It is also important to note here that a large amount of iron slag was found from this site.

Another stone factory is located at the site of Markhan right above the Umiam stream. The debris consisted of waste flakes which have been artificially piled up in large heaps by the recent cultivators while clearing the area for cultivation on the slopes of the hill (Plate 15). An observation made from a section of the lower part of the slope, shows that there is a very thick layer of accumulated waste-flakes and cores in the spot. This seems to indicate the extent of occupation of this place as a factory site. No trace of other archaeological evidences was however recovered from the area.

Unfinished Tools

<u>Plate No. 15</u>

Not a single finished or ground implement was found from the site although this is the biggest factory site so far encountered in the region. Large numbers of unfinished tools along with waste flakes and cores have been recovered from the site. No effort was made to classify the unfinished varieties since they belong to the same industry with the rest found in Umiam-Barapani, Umjajew and San Mer (Upper Shillong).

The Site of Tynring (See Fig. 12 for Reference)

Location
District: East Khasi Hills District. Meghalaya
1200-1400 m above Sea Level.
Physiographic Position: Upland

This site is the name of a village which lies north of the Umkhen stream and east of Shillong. The site overlooks the Ri-Bhoi low land from a much higher elevation. Preliminary survey of the site led to the finding of a single finished shouldered tool from the surface of an old road close to a perennial spring near an expansive stretch of paddy fields. The site shows great potential for uncovering Neolithic material as it is located close to the Umkhen stream and the Ri-Bhoi lowlands. The elderly people of the village have a different term for these stone tools and they called them *Maw Shrieh* or Monkey stone. Large amount of iron slag was found scattered throughout the modern settlement which certainly proves that the area had attracted Neolithic habitation and the occupation of this area continued to the period when iron came into common use. Large numbers of Megalithic monuments are also found around the periphery of the village.

Finished: Ground

Plate No: 11

Shape	Type	Raw Material	Maximum size in Cm. LxBxT.	Description
Rectangular	Shouldered	Amphibolite	6 x 5.2 x 1 cm	The shoulders are finely cut but not perfectly at right angles to the tenon. The tenon is square and relatively large compared with the body. The cutting edge is highly beveled, produced by unifacial grinding and the sides are ground flat.

The Sites around Shiliang Myntang–Chei Bnai

<u>Location</u>
District: Jaintia Hills District. Meghalaya
<u>Physiographic Position: Low Land</u>

This is the only site recorded from Jaintia hills. It lies on the border of Ri-Bhoi district and close to the Karbi Anglong district of Assam. Two stone implements were collected from this area. One was collected close to the Mynriang stream a tributary of the Myntang River under the Shilliang Myntang Dalloiship[37]. The tool from this spot was unearthed when the local people were hunting for mountain rats approximately 4 feet below the surface. Another stone implement was collected from a village called Cheibnai about 2.5 Km from the Mynriang stream under the Shilliang Myntang Daloiship. The tool was recovered during the laying of a section of a paddy field and was found 3.6 feet below the surface. The site has the potential of producing more Neolithic implements as the locals claim that they have found plenty of such implements at different places across the area. A more concentrated field work around this entire zone would certainly yield more Neolithic evidence. As this site is geographically located between the Ri-Bhoi, Jaintia hills and Karbi Anglong district, it can add further scope in understanding the relationship between Neolithic sites of Assam, especially those of Cachar and Karbi Anglong districts with those found in the Khasi and Jaintia hills.

Classification of Tools from Shiliang Myntang-Chei Bnai Sites (Plate 9)

<u>Finished Tools: Ground</u>

Shape	Type	Raw Material	Maximum size in Cm. LxBxT.	Description
Rectangular	Adze	Amphibol ite	8x4x1.8	A facetted tool with parallel sides with slight shoulders that slopes from the tenon towards the body at an acute angle. The sides are ground flat. The cutting edge highly beveled, produced through unifacial grinding.
Triangular	Tanged	Shale	8x7x1	There is a slight grinding at the shoulders thereby showing a tenon at the butt. The sides are ground flat and the cutting edge median produced through equal bifacial grinding.

---

[37]Doloiship is an autonomous administrative unit in Jaintia hills in the local administration.

The Site of Nongspung (Fig. 11)

<u>Location</u>
District: West Khasi Hills District. Meghalaya
Physiographic Position: Upland

This site lies in the West Khasi hills district, classed in this research as a site of the upland region. It is located close to the Nongspung stream also known as *Langrei* stream. The site is named after a village which was the headquarters of the Nongspung chieftainship. The village itself is traditionally known for its specialisation in iron working and it has become the centre of the iron industry in the west Khasi hills. Traces of iron working are found throughout the length and breadth of the village. The elderly people of the village are well acquainted with the concept of Thunder Axe or *Sdie Pyrthat*. They reported the finding of such axes from different parts of the village during the course of their cultivation, but owing to their ignorance and also fear of thunder strikes, threw away these stone axes whenever they found them. During a brief course of survey of the area an axe was recovered from the house of an old man name Kodri Syiemlieh (Plate 21), who reported to have found the axe from a hill slope near the present village a place which he claimed was the earlier settlement of the people of Nongspung village. This site lies on the border of the East Khasi hills and owing to such proximity there is enough ground to prove that the Neolithic people had also exploited this part of the hills. Quite a good number of Megalithic monuments hewn from granite are erected along the site and the settlement area.

Classification of Tool from Nongspung Site (Plate 12A)

<u>Finished Tool: Ground</u>

Figure. No.	Shape	Type	Raw Material	Maximum size in Cm. LxBxT.	Description
Not Drawn	Triangular	Axe (wedge)	Amphibolite	9x5.4x1	A pointed-butt axe with sides and butt end ground perfectly flat. The cross section bi-convex. The cutting edge median, produced by equal bifacial grinding.

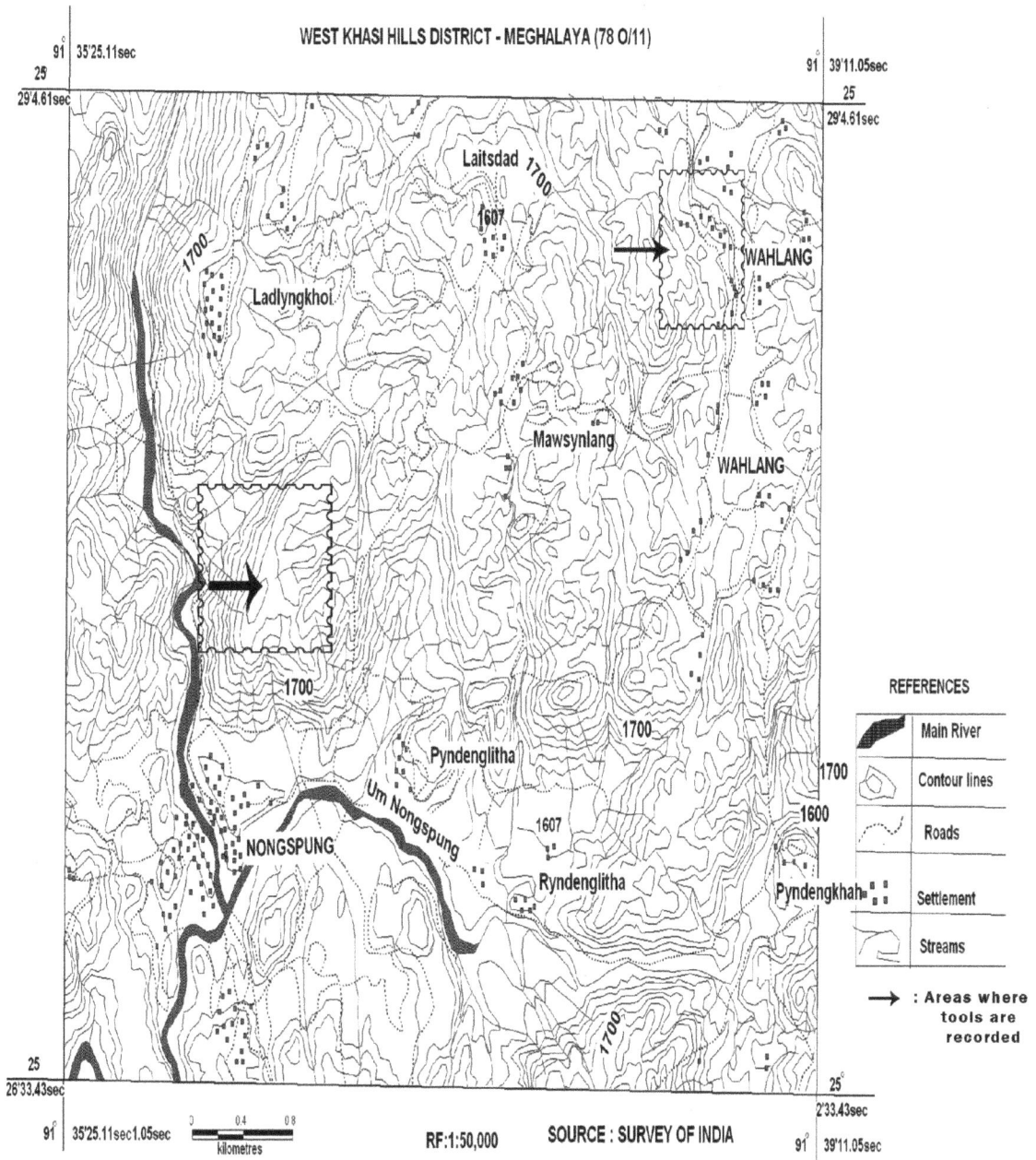

WEST KHASI HILLS DISTRICT - MEGHALAYA (78 O/11)

REFERENCES

	Main River
	Contour lines
	Roads
	Settlement
	Streams
→	: Areas where tools are recorded

RF:1:50,000   SOURCE : SURVEY OF INDIA

Figure 11: Topographic Settings of Nongspung and Wahlang Sites

The Site of Wahlang (Fig. 11 for Reference)

Location
District: West Khasi Hills District. Meghalaya
Physiographic Position: Upland

This site lies in the West Khasi hills also in the upland region. It lies opposite to the Nongspung village separated by the Nongspung stream or the *Langrei* stream. The older generations of people from the village are well acquainted with the concept of Thunder Axe or *Sdie Pyrthat* as it is locally known. The people reported finding such axes from their fields during cultivation, but owing to their ignorance and also fear of thunder strike they threw away these stone axes whenever they found them. During a brief course of survey of the area an axe was recovered from the house of another old man name Lyngdoh Kynshi who recovered the axe while digging a paddy field.

Finished Tools: Ground

Plate No: 12 B

Shape	Type	Raw Material	Maximum size in Cm. LxBxT.	Description
Triangular	Axe	Amphibolite	8.2x5x.8	Another Pointed axe with sides and top ground flat. The cross section is slightly bi-convex. The cutting edge is symmetrical and median produced by equal bifacial grinding.

CHAPTER 6

ANALYSIS OF FINDS

Overview

The present investigation conducted field work over major parts of Ri-Bhoi, the East Khasi hills, the West Khasi hills and the Jaintia hills districts of the Central Meghalaya Plateau. As a result, of this investigation numbers of Neolithic sites with immense potential for further investigation were uncovered. With the aim to achieve some insights into the dispersal and location pattern of the Neolithic settlements in the region under-study the sites were recorded and plotted in maps. The general picture that emerged out of these field investigations confirms that, the Neolithic sites throughout the area under-study is scattered unevenly showing wide degree of variation in the level of concentration. Neolithic evidences. The physiographic, vegetation and climatic conditions are seen to be the major influential factor which controls the concentration of Neolithic population in some areas of the region.

All the sites recorded in this research were considered on the basis of findings of stone artifacts recovered from surface collections. Not a single stone implement or other object was retrieved from an undisturbed or stratified context. It thus, made it impossible to establish a chronological horizon about the Neolithic evidences on the basis of their contexts. In the concluding chapter of this research, however, an effort has been made to arrive with some form of hypotheses to show the different stages of Neolithic occupation of various parts of the region. This was done so with an aim to

understand the movement of the Neolithic folks within the area under study in relative terms.

Sites

Based on the different localities from where the stone implements were collected, a total number of 19 sites were indentified along the Khasi, Ri-Bhoi and Jaintia hills of the central Meghalaya plateau. All the sites catalogue in this research have not produced ceramic evidences, and whatever traces of potteries that occur alongside with the Neolithic stone implements came from some sites only.

The following are the different sites the names of which are listed according to their localities or villages mentioned in the map:

1. 9 sites are located in the Ri-Bhoi region identified in this research project as low-lands.

2. 5 sites were found on the East Khasi hills identified in this research project as uplands.

3. 2 sites are located in Jaintia hills both lying very close to the Ri- Bhoi low -lands.

4. 3 sites are discovered in the West Khasi hills identified in this research here as upland zone.

Except for the one site of Umiam-Barapani, which has already been reported by earlier investigators, the rest of the sites mentioned in this research were discovered during the course of this investigation.

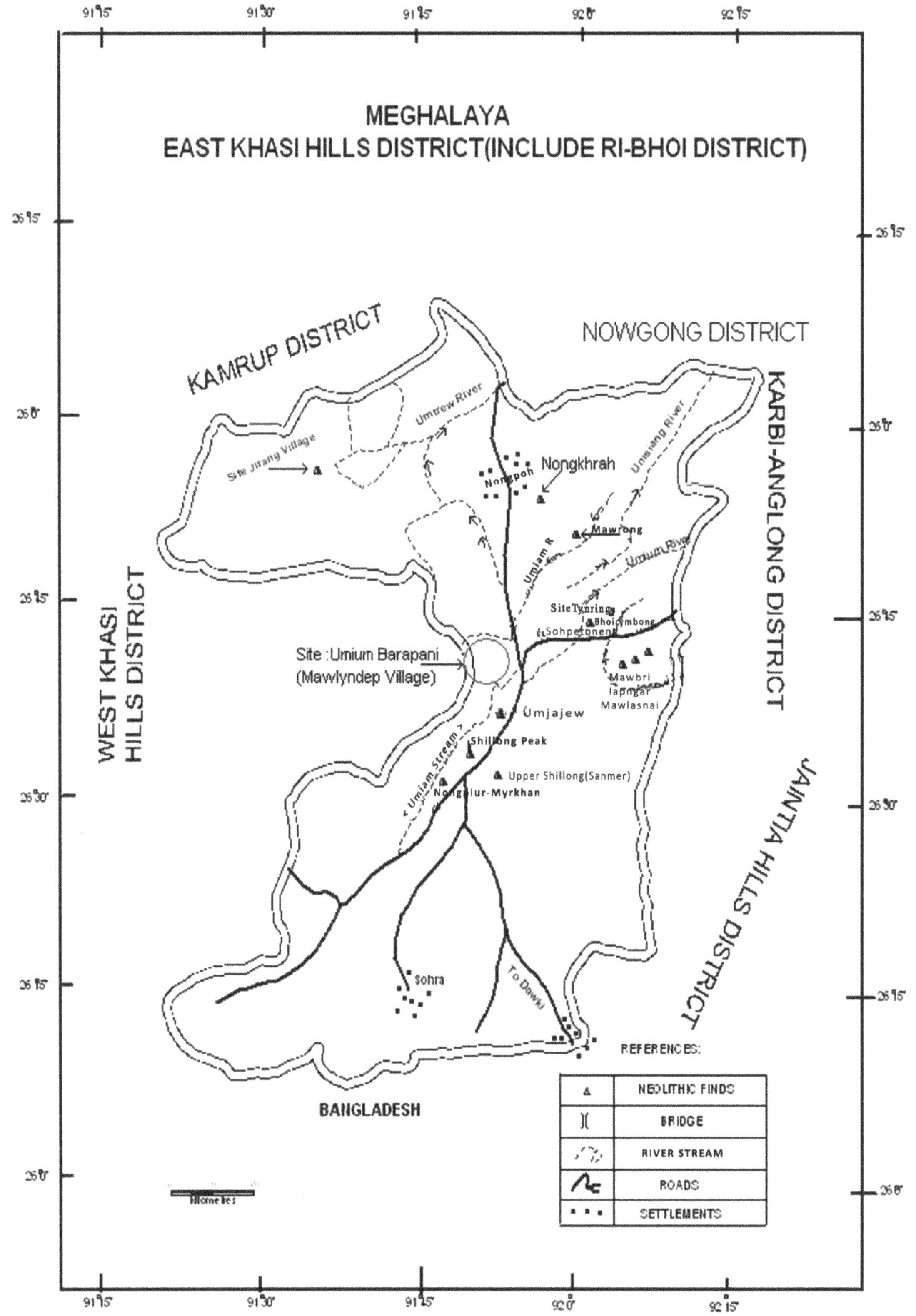

Figure 12: Sites in East Khasi Hills District (including Ri-Bhoi District)

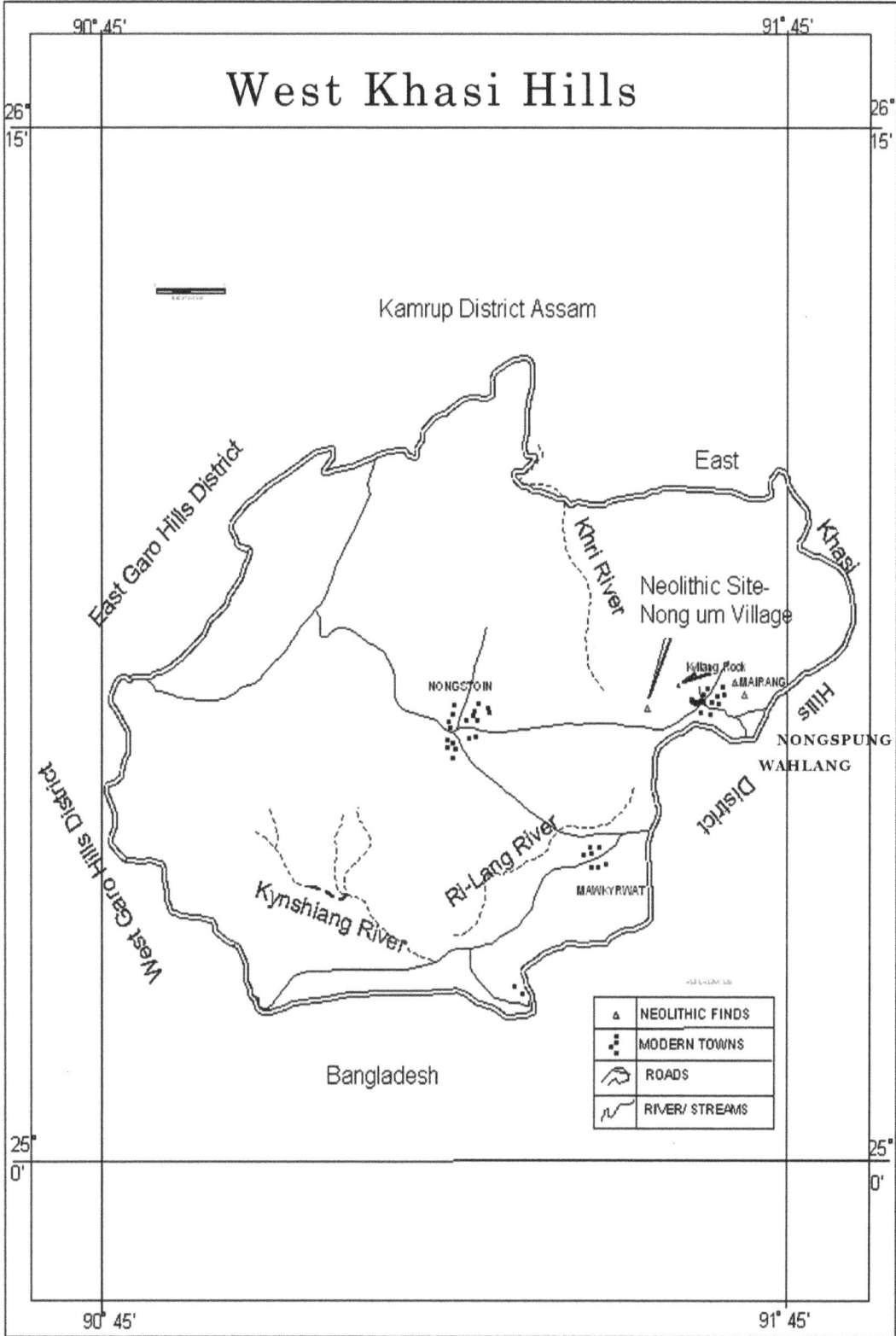

Figure 13: Sites in West Khasi Hills District

Artifacts

A total of 94 Nos. of tools which have been classed as finished category, were collected and studied in this research project. On the basis of their types, they are classified as:

Types	Total Numbers
Shouldered	18
Tanged	11
Axe	36
Adze	26
Total	91

Sites where Stone Implements recorded

Site	Shouldered	Tanged	Axe	Adze	Total
Umiam	04	08	12	09	33
Sohpet Bneng	04	00	03	04	11
Mawrong	05	00	07	01	13
Mawbri	03	00	05	01	09
Iapngar areas	01	01	04	02	08
Tyrso areas	00	00	01	05	06
Nongkhrah	00	00	00	01	01
Umjajew	00	01	01	01	03
Upper Shillong	00	00	01	01	02
Tynring	01	00	00	00	01
Shiliang Myntang-Chei Bnai areas	00	01	00	01	02
Nongspung	00	00	01	00	01
Wahlang	00	00	01	00	01
Total	18	11	36	26	91

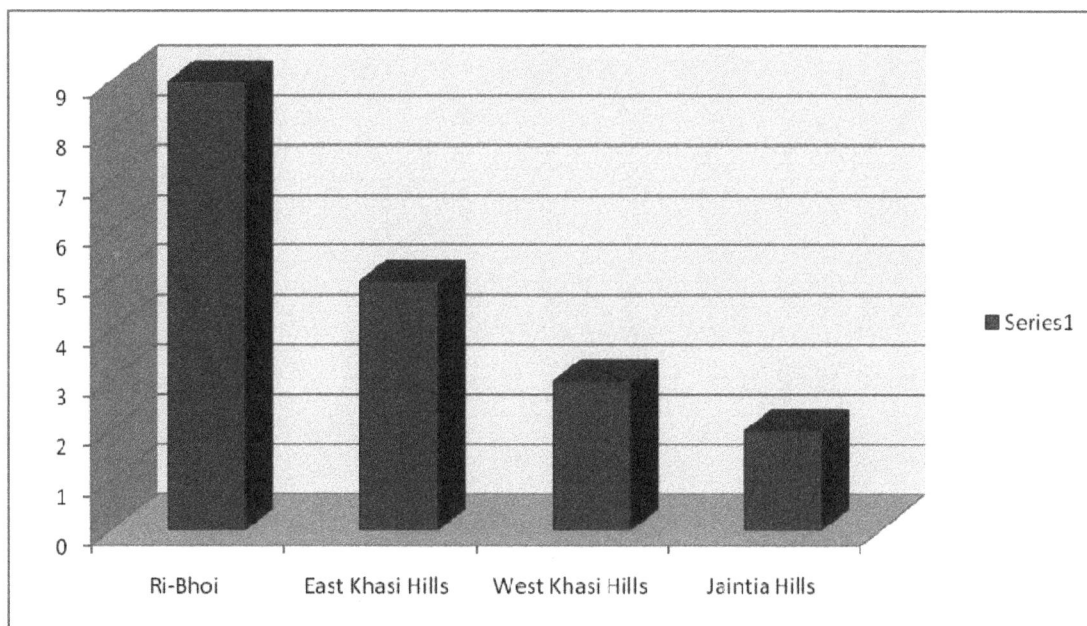

Figure 14: Graphic representation of Sites' Distribution in Area of Study

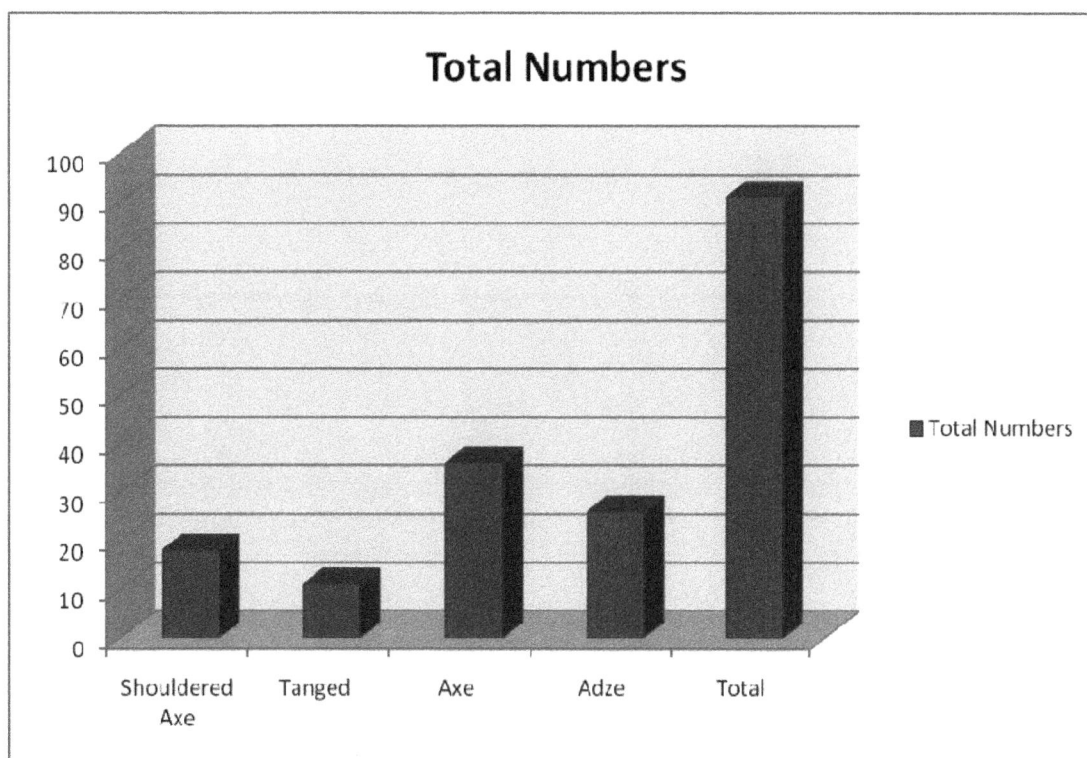

Figure 15: Graphic representation of Tool Distribution from Study Area

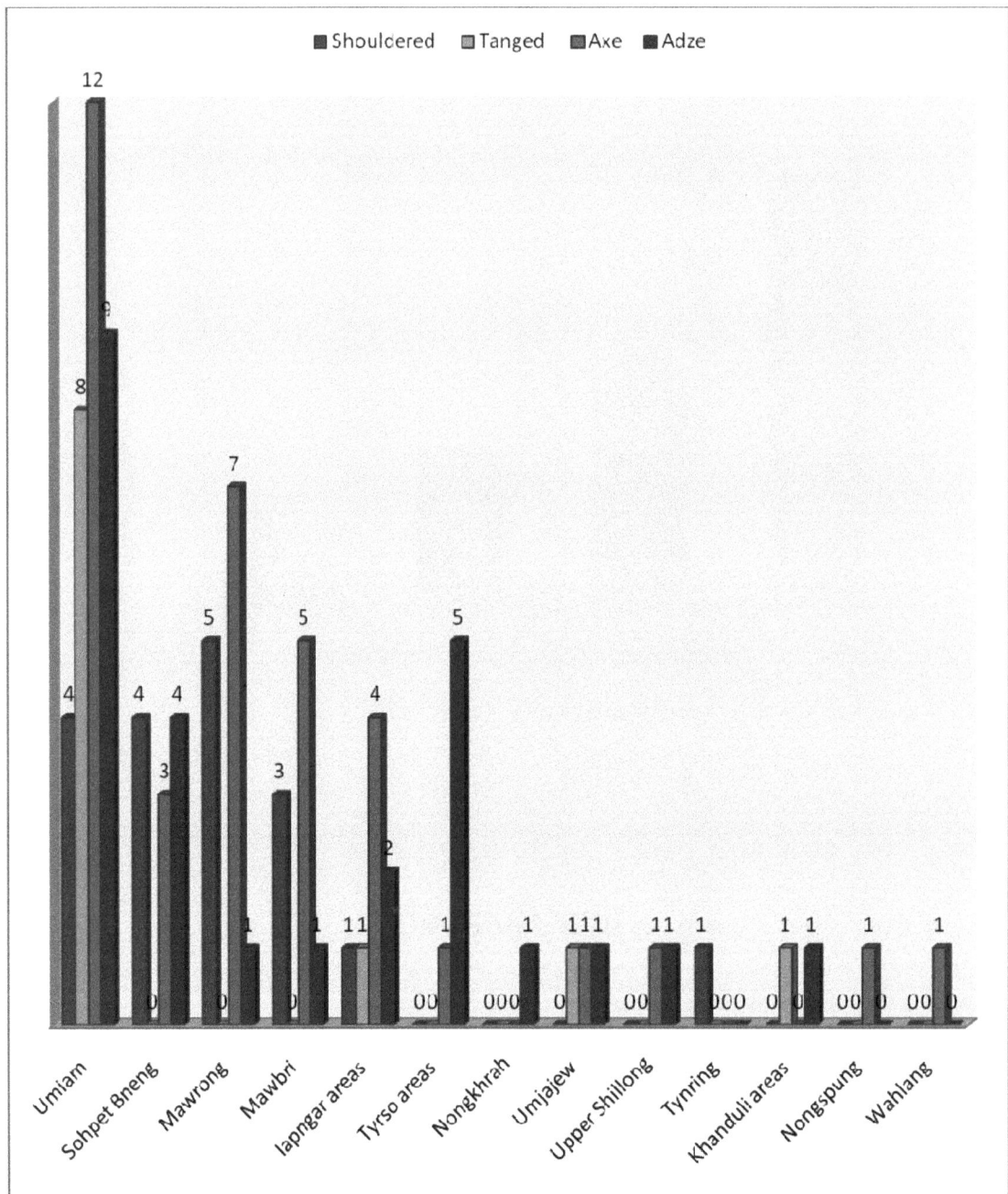

Figure 16: Graphic representation of Un-Ground Implements from Area of Study

More than 50 Numbers of stone implements which are classed in this research as 'unfinished' or 'un-ground' were also studied (Plate 18). The tools in this category were recovered only from four sites and they were found along with considerable number of stone debris which included waste flakes and cores. In the reduction sequence model most of these unfinished implements fall within the early bi-face and late bi-face manufacturing stage. Such implements have attained their desired shape,

but there are no trace of them being ground or polished in any form and hence, completely devoid of a working edge. These are the types of stone implements which typologically resembles pre-Neolithic tools. If found in isolation, such stone implements (especially the large type of unfinished tools under the classification chapter) could have been easily mistaken for pre-Neolithic implements because of their primary stage of manufacturing. But as they are found in association with ground tools and unground shouldered tools, their cultural association with the pre-Neolithic level cannot be authenticate till more research can be undertaken. Most of the tools in this category that were collected from the area under-study were flaked from amphibolite material and some from slate. The raw material was used for all stone implements recorded throughout the study region are made from locally available material which shows some regional variations. Amphibolite was used for most of the tools from Khasi uplands, whereas slate, indurated shale and sandstone were used for tools from Ri-Bhoi low lands. There are few exceptional specimens made of carbonaceous quartzite found in the upland zone.

The recovery of three unfinished shouldered tools, one from the site of Umjajew and two from the site of Umiam-Barapani (Plate 18.C), strong ground to prove that these shouldered implements belong to the same set of unfinished

industry and certainly help to provide better analogy about the antiquity of the entire industry of unfinished tools as recorded from all the four sites of the study area. Based on their association to the context from where they have been recorded, it may be safely concluded for now that these unfinished implements do not belong to an older or pre-Neolithic cultural level as cited by earlier scholars. All the tools in this category have attained their desired shapes but there is no trace of a working edge or grinding in any form. They were left unfinished probably discarded without use.

On the basis of their types and probable indication of functions, the unfinished tools are categorized into four types:

E. Quadrangular
F. Shouldered/Tanged
G. Pointed Butt Axe
H. Round Butt Axe

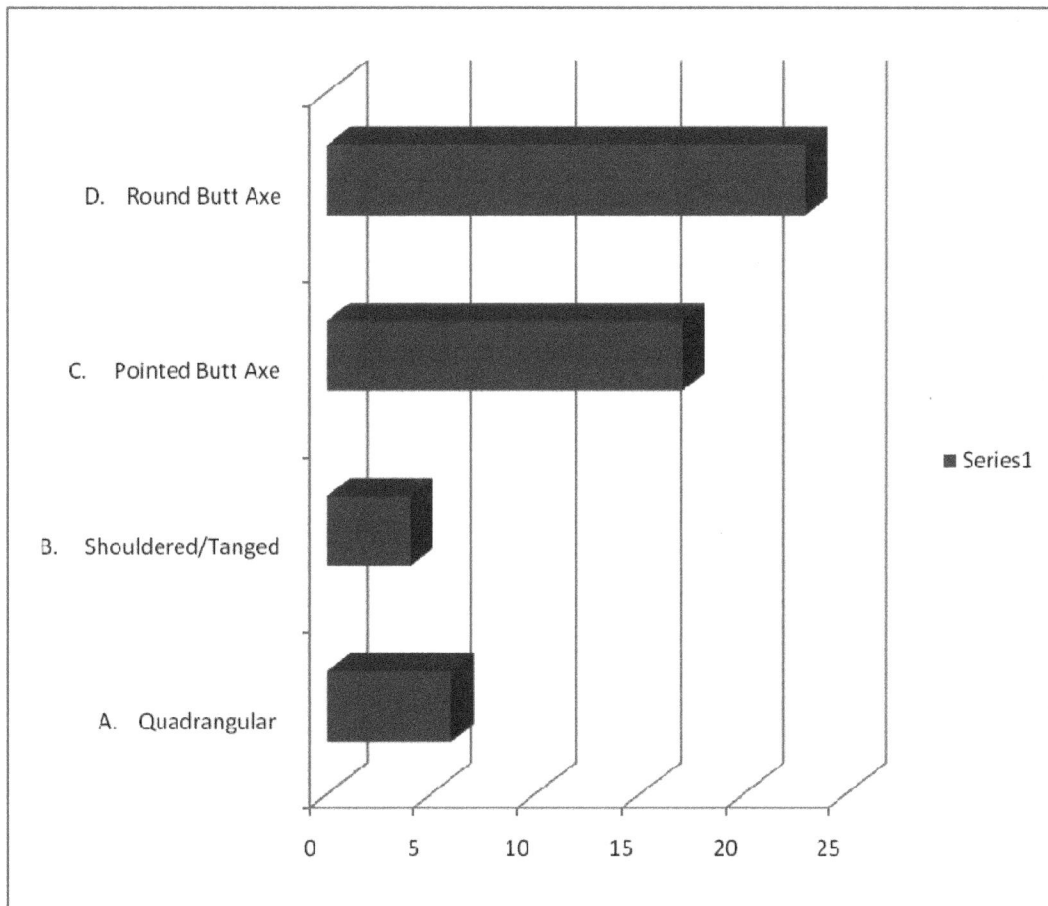

Figure 17: Graphic Representation of Un-ground Implements from area under study

Nature of Preservation of Stone implements

The climatic condition of this region is characterised mainly by heavy rainfall and a humid and moist atmospheric condition in the summer. The acidic level of the soil in the uplands due to the presence of pine forest (5±2 ph). The acidic condition of Ri-Bhoi and Jaintia hills low lands is mild because of the dense concentration of broad leaf forest (7± ph). Owing to the said factors, the nature of preservation of stone implements is very low and this is seen mainly on stone implements recovered from the uplands zone which shows a thick tinge of patination on all of them. The level of patina is observed mostly on stone implements which made of amphibolite material, a major rock type for making stone tools throughout the uplands of Khasi hills in particular. The patina on all these stone implements is grayish to black in colour. The level of patina is less with tools from other materials like slate or shale, which are found in higher percentage from the Ri-Bhoi lowlands and lesser from the uplands zone.

Synthesis of the Data

The waste flake and cores are generally recorded in large numbers and were occasionally found to have been piled together in small mounds by cultivators (Plate 15). The amount of unfinished stone implements does throw some light about the functional purpose of the sites. On the basis of the accumulation level of stone debris, these sites were perhaps stable factory sites that have been used for a fairly long period of time. The stone implements were probably discarded or left unfinished by the stone workers as a huge chunk of waste flake and cores were found at the sites of Barapani, Umjajew, Upper-Shillong San-Mer and Nongpyuir-Myrkhan, thus clearly indicating that these sites had assumed a status of being factory centers specializing in stone tool manufacturing for a fairly long period of time (Plate 13.B). The sites of Barapani, Umjajew, Upper-Shillong San Mer and Nongpyuir Myrkhan bears similar characteristic feature of being factory sites during the Neolithic period and the basic material used for manufacturing stone tools is amphibolites. The source of the material is found all along the Khasi hills as intrusive rock. It is also possible to understand on the basis of the technology adopted, that these sites represent a single cultural phase as they are found within an approximate area of 20 to 25 Sq Km. It can be further speculated that these sites have probably specialised in production of stone tools whose supply may have reached throughout the length and breadth of the Khasi and Jaintia hills during the Neolithic and late-Neolithic times. The ethnographic data further shows that these very same areas represents areas which have also specialized in traditional iron production in the past, traces of the iron industry is still seen today.

One implement recovered from the site of Nongkhrah (Plate 14.1) from Ri-Bhoi district needs special mention, since it is the most unusual from the entire stone tools assemblage collected from the region under study. This tool resembles the *facetted tool with side notches* type describe by Dani that was found from Naga Hills (Dani, 1960,p 63) and the *notches type* recorded by T.C. Sharma from Rongchangiri of Garo hills (Sankalaia, 1962 p.289). The stone tools recovered from the localities of Tyrso and the adjoining villages very close to the plains of Assam are also important from the point of view of their typology. Five of the six tools made of slate are flat celts, the types of which that are not encountered much in the interior parts of the plateau except for those that was reported by Godwin-Austin from Shillong (Godwin-Austin, 1975, p.158). These types form the majority in the tool assemblages from the different sites of Garo hills (A total of 350 nos.) (Sankalaia, 1962, p.297). The recovery of these tools especially from the sites lying on the outline parts of Ri-Bhoi surely attest to the importance of Ri-Bhoi as a region which disseminated Neolithic technology not only towards the Khasi and Jaintia hills, but also as an area of attraction that probably bridged the Neolithic technology of region under study with that of Garo hills.

The raw material of the entire stone tool industry of the Khasi and Jaintia hills in the

Neolithic period can be easily identified on the basis of three types; Amphibolite of khasi green stone, Slate and Shale, the first one being used more widely than the rest especially in the Khasi upland zone. A single specimen of long variety of shouldered Adze recovered from the site of Mawbri in Ri-Bhoi district, which is made of a highly polished amphibolite (Plate 9.1) and this specimen is unique from the entire collection both in terms of the size and preservation.

Dispersion of Sites

The archaeological evidences of the Neolithic culture from the study area, clearly revealed that the northern part of the central Meghalaya plateau, or the Ri-Bhoi region can be recognized as the area of greatest attraction as far as the Neolithic settlement in the study region is concerned. The Ri-Bhoi region which is primarily characterized by undulating hills and valleys, with sub-tropical vegetation and moist climate produced the highest number of Neolithic evidences in the form of finished stone implements and few fragmented potsherds which were collected and reported from various jhum fields all along this region.

As already mentioned above, since the aim of this research is to understand the dispersal of Neolithic elements in to the Khasi and Jaintia hills and as much of the artefacts were collected from the surface or from very disturbed contexts, no effort has been made to understand the chronological and temporal context of the Neolithic culture in the region under study. However serious effort is made on the field to understand and associate the Neolithic artifacts in the light of other supporting evidences such as folklores, oral tradition, iron slag evidence and the Megalithic monuments. With an aim to understand the movement pattern of the Neolithic folk within the region under study, a hypothesis has been forwarded in this research to form linkages among the different Neolithic sites found so far, and to understand the Neolithic situation of this area as a single entity.

Mentioned must be made here, that on the basis of the tools recovered and raw materials used,

there seems to be a clear indication that the people who arrived in the Khasi and Jaintia hills have already equipped themselves with Neolithic technology which they brought in from outside. The context of stone tool debris from the various sites of the upland zone, seems to indicate that it was a late phase of Neolithic culture which flourished in the areas along the upland zones. Such a situation is seen clearly on the tools found from the sites of Upper-Shillong Sanmer, Umjajew, and Nongpyuir Myrkhan, where the evidence of waste flakes and cores were found barely 15 cm from the surface. Nothing however can be speculated in a similar manner for other sites since there is no data for correlation, except for the finished implements that were found on the surface of tilled fields. But from the site of Shiliang Myntang-Chei Bnai of Jaintia hills, the two stone implements that collected from the region were recovered from a relatively deeper layer about four feet from the surface. This may probably indicate that the site must have been much earlier especially if we consider its proximity to the North Cachar hills from where the Neolithic elements from the site of Deojali Hading could have easily penetrated. The site of Barapani-Umiam may probably be treated as older than the rest of the sites found in the interior parts of the Khasi hills but it has to be noted that this assumption is not built on the basis of the tool technology which some scholars (Medhi,1990, p.39) have speculated to be of the pre-Neolithic (as already mentioned above they belong to the unfinished stage of the Stone tools) but rather on the basis of the context of some of the tools which are found in the layer **(Plate 3)**. The C-14 dates from the site of Marakdola on the northern border of the Khasi hills which is dated to 1292 A.D (Rao,1977 p.202) can be applied for the later phase of the Neolithic industry of this region especially the upland zones of the central Meghalaya Plateau.

A large proportion of the findings in this research are based mainly on the stone implements that were already exposed on the surface because of either artificial disturbance like jhum cultivation or because of the natural erosion of the covering soil. The impact of the former condition is far more common in the area of field study since the practice of shifting cultivation although on the wane state yet still very common, especially in the Ri-Bhoi region where regeneration of vegetation is very fast owing to the fertility of the soil. Only at the site of Umiam-Barapani that a slight evidence of disturbance of the site was caused by the earlier cultivation of the area and the seasonal impact of the recurring water pressure from the artificial lake which gradually exposed the embedded stone tools[38].

It is on the basis of the archaeological evidence derived from such context as described above that the degree of profusion in the occurrences of stone tool, have been tabulated in order to work out the pattern of the spread and concentration of the Neolithic sites around the study region. As already mentioned, the archaeological findings combined with ethnographic information are sure pointers that the concentration of finished stone tools remain highest on the northern belt of the study area i.e. the Ri-Bhoi region along the Umiam, Umkhen and Myntang Rivers. The evidences of stone tool collection slowly decreases in intensity towards the central upland zone and are found to be completely absent in all the areas along the southern precipitous zones of the Khasi hills commonly known as the *War* area (Figure 18).

The evidence of stone tools is sparsely recorded from the central and western part of the central Meghalaya plateau. On the basis of the evidence recorded from the types, raw material used and the technology adopted, the stone implements collected from the sites that are located in the central region of the area of research (termed as the Khasi uplands in this paper), reveal a direct extension of the Neolithic culture of the northern Ri-Bioi. But since, no dates of any form can be calibrated archaeologically it is not possible to bring out the differences in chronological order of the sites from the various parts of the area under-study.

The southern precipitous zones of the study region has not produce any form of Neolithic evidence either as tools, potsherds or archaeological object or any other sources which can be ethnographically and distinctively associated with the Neolithic culture. Until some form of archaeologicalevidences surface up in the future, it is safe to conclude at this stage that the southern precipitous zone of the study region locally known as the *War* region of the central Meghalaya plateau did not attract the movement of people during the Neolithic period. Although the *War* region is fairly rich in flora and fauna that would have necessarily attracted early slash and burnt cultivators, the absence of Neolithic evidences from the region could be due to its rocky land mass which does not allow the faster regeneration of vegetation, a condition necessary for slash and burnt cultivation.

In Jaintia hills, the Neolithic evidences are concentrated around the eastern part of the region close to the direction of Cachar hills where the site of Neolithic site of Daojali Hading is located. Two important sites were recorded from this region, one in Shiliang Myntang-Chei Bnai and another from Saipung. Both these sites are located close to the Ri-Bhoi low lands with vegetational, climatic and physiographic characteristics similar to that of the latter. Although only two stone implements were recovered from this zone, the ethnographic survey of the area clearly indicates the potential presence of many more Neolithic sites in the region especially around the areas close to the Kopli river. But due the dense forest which covers these areas, it is not possible to undertake an extensive fieldwork of the region and hence, archaeologically data cannot be tested. No sites were however recorded from the interior parts of the central plateau of Jaintia hills. Similar to the situation in Khasi hills, the Neolithic habitation of Jaintia hills is concentrated only along the areas close to Cachar hills and Ri-Bhoi region, hypothetically, the very areas from where the Neolithic technology probably made its inroads into the Khasi and Jaintia hills from the eastward movement (See Figure 19).

---

[38] These were also in already disturbed context as they were found mainly on ridges which were form because of cultivation of the area before the artificial lake was constructed.

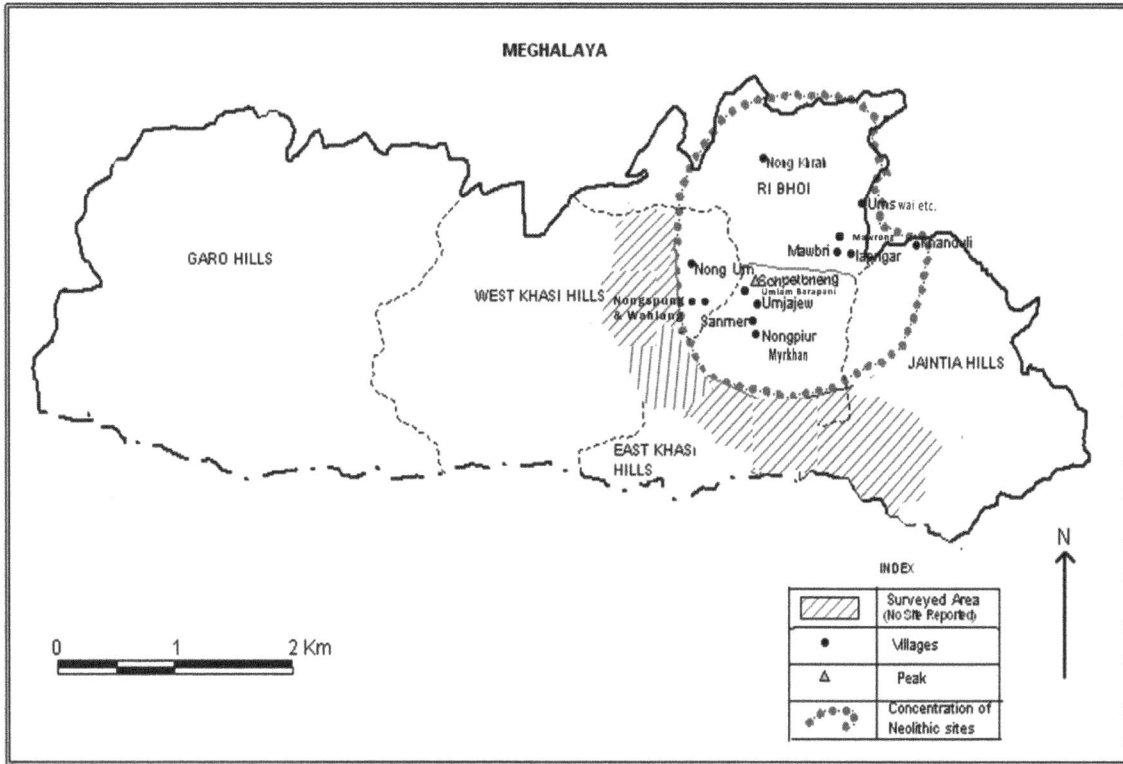

Figure 18: Distribution of Sites in Khasi-Jaintia Hills

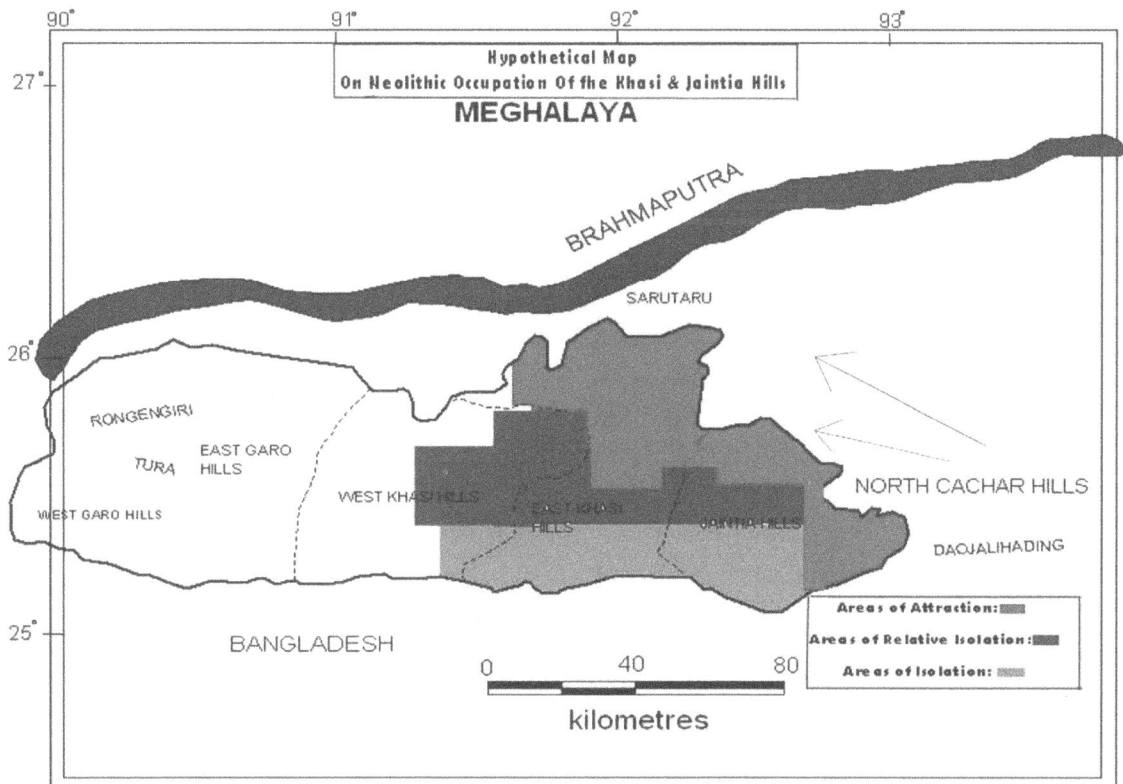

Figure 19: Hypothetical Map on Neolithic Occupation of Khasi-Jaintia Hills

Other Archaeological Objects

A total number of 10 Ring stones in broken form were collected from the site of Umiam-Barapni during the course of this research (Plate 6). These ring stones were found from a flat face of a hillock from an area within 100sq feet approximately. This particular spot lies very close to the erstwhile Umiam stream. The size of these ring stones, are not uniform and the diameter of the disc range from a maximum of 13.3cm to a minimum diameter of 5.7cm. All of these are made from slate material. The use of these ring stones was certainly associated to adding weight for a particular implement which could be used weights for mace[39] or digging stick or fishing nets and least of all spindle[40]. The presence of these ring stones at Umiam-Barapani site had added significantly to the variety of the existing evidence from the site and therefore help to provide a more comprehensive understanding of the site in the context of the Neolithic culture of the region under study especially when such evidence have not been recorded from any other site within the area under study. The nearest site so far in the Northeast India, from where ring stones have been recorded by M.C. Goswani from Garo hills (Sharma, 2002, pp. 465-484)

The presence of the clay pellets at the surface of Umaim-Barapani site certainly points to some degree of cultural affinity between the site of Umiam Barapani and the site of Marakdola, from where similar clay pellets were also recorded by the excavator from Layer III of the excavation occurring in the same cultural horizon with the corded potteries. The date 1292 AD, assigned to the site of the post-Neolithic Marakdola site may also be applied to the later phase of Neolithic culture of Umaim-Barapani site after considering the state of preservation of these clay objects in a site like Umaim-Barapani.

---

[39]The uniform beveling along the side of the outer ring is also suited for aerodynamic performance which may probably add to the function of the ring stones as weights for a wooden or bamboo spear.
[40]Such assumption is made because of the variety in their sizes recoded from a single spot.

In the collection of the archaeological objects recovered, few samples of potsherds were also recorded from the sites of Sohpet Bneng, Barapani and Upper-Shillong-Sanmer. Most of the ceramic evidences reflected the characteristic feature of the Neolithic pottery technology of the region. All the sherd pieces are hand-made and are fired at a very low temperature as evident from the bigger space of the dark core at the section profile of the potsherds. They are of mostly dull chocolate-brown in colour and made from very coarse quality of clay. The clay was heavily tempered with quartz grits, which are prominently evident on the outer surface of the sherds (Plate 7). The sherd pieces bear cord-impressed patterns on the outer surface caused by the beater and pad method, a characteristic feature of the pottery technology in the region. All the potsherds are found close to the spot where the stone implements are recovered. Two wheel-made pots in partially fragmentary stage were found from Umiam-Barapani, but these certainly belong to the later cultural phase of the site, since this site itself was continuously occupied till the construction of the lake in 1964 (Plate 8).

Cultural transitional phase in the Study Area

The course of the Umiam stream acted as land mark for the movement of the people between the Ri-Bhoi region and Khasi uplands. The sites with high concentration of stone tools or waste flakes evidences like Sohpet Bneng, Umiam-Barapani, Umjajew, San Mer and Nongpyiur-Myrkhan are located very close to the Umiam stream. Thus, with so much archaeological evidence, the importance of the Umiam stream in the moulding of the Neolithic culture of the Khasi hills is definitely unquestioned.

The stone assemblages recovered from the site of Umiam-Barapani which produce diverse typology and quite a large number of both finished and un-ground or unfinished tools, explain the role of this site in the context of the Neolithic culture of the entire area under study. The density of stone evidence collected from the site also reflect the habitational level of this site as fairly large and expansive. This site was definitely a settlement area since large numbers of stone tools in their usable stages, fragments of potteries and a remarkable number of ring stones are found dispersed uniformly around the site. Probably the Neolithic settlements of the Umaim-Barapani are located on the hillocks around this stream, most of which are submerged under the present lake and its surrounding hills. The site of Sohpet Bneng which is at a much higher altitude probably represents one among the sites of Umiam-Barapani. The sites of Umjajew, San-Mer and Nongpyiur-Myrkhan on its south are largely the extension of the Umiam-Barapani site. These evidences revealed the importance of the Umiam-Barapani site in the context of the Neolithic culture of the Khasi hills in particular and the region under study at large. This site may well be the kernel of a very stable Neolithic phase in the Khasi hills which continued right up to the recent past.

Regional Variations in raw material of Stone Tools

There is a clear variation in the choice of raw material use for manufacturing stone implement. The choice is probably determined by the availability of raw material. Slate, indurated shale, amphibolite and sandstone are found to be the dominant rock types used by Neolithic people of the Ri-Bhoi region, where as Amphibolite is more common in the Khasi uplands. The sites of Umiam-Barapani and Sohpet Bneng represents all types of raw material but a high percentage of the unfinished and un-ground implements are mostly fashioned out of amphibolite. The amphibolite material as already mentioned, are covered with a fair amount of patina which gives a clay-like impression on the tools when observed from the surface. It is rather not very clear at this level of research to explain the absence of patination on tools made from other materials besides amphibolite. The acidic nature of the soil in the uplands could be the only factor if we consider that the Neolithic culture of this entire study area fall within the same chronological horizon. If other factors should be considered, it will only come till absolute date can be taken from the various sites of the region.

Ethnographic parallel on hafting-technique of Shouldered Implements

It is generally held that while in operation, most of the Neolithic tools are hafted to a wooden handle-shaft. How are these tools hafted is however yet to be understood since not a single stone implement having a handle attached to it has been recovered from an archaeological context. Ethnographic information derived from some of the older people from the area of research, claimed that these tools are hafted to a wood or a bamboo shaft using hard vine (Genus: *Diosorea*) or thin-sliced bamboo- bark, as tying material. Although such a method cannot be ruled out, there is however, no living evidence of such a practice ever reported. Using modern day ethnographic parallel, the method for hafting the iron hoe, which is considered to be a iron replica of the shouldered stone implement may give some insight about the hafting technique. The Khasi hoe which is commonly used for agriculture are of two forms (Plates 22.3-4): 1)M*ohkhiew heh* or the Big hoe 2)*Mohkhiew rit* or small hoe. The tenon of the big hoe is first inserted into an iron socket which is then inserted into a wooden shaft, while the tenon of the small hoe is directly inserted into the end part of a bamboo root that has a natural occurring shape of a golf stick, as a shaft. In function the big hoe is used for turning up the hard soil, while the small one is use for loosening the soil into smaller parts in order to make it soft. In the context of the evolution of this technology, the small hoe appear to have retained much of its prototype form, while the big hoe seems to have undergone modification because of the malleability of iron. The angle between the tenon and the shaft of the big hoe is conventionally less than right angles, while in the case of the small hoe it is normally at right angle. While in operation, the acute angle (between the shaft and the blade) of the big hoe allows it to slice and turn up the soil a lot easier. On the other hand the right angle (between the shaft and the blade) in the case of the small hoe becomes useful only for digging a straight section into the soil and is generally use only on softer soil which has been either worked by the big hoe or on soil that had been soften due to burning.

Thus drawing from ethnographic parallel, the tenon of the shouldered tool was probably inserted rather than tied to the shaft. It may be proposed that, the beveled working edge shouldered implements provided the acute angle necessary to achieve the slicing objective as in the case of the big hoe, while the median cutting edge tools may have been used for cutting or digging in a straight section as in the case of the small hoe.

CHAPTER 7

A PROFILE ON THE NEOLITHIC CULTURE OF KHASI- JAINTIA HILLS

Spread of Neolithic Settlement

It has to be noted at the beginning of this chapter, that the Neolithic evidences in the form of finished stone implements recovered from the region under study are mainly concentrated in the Ri-Bhoi region close to Jaintia hills. The profusion of stone tool evidences is highest around the northern part of the Ri-Bhoi region along the border of Karbi Anglong district of southern part Brahmaputra valley of Assam. This result is highly crucial from the point of understanding the intra-hills migration pattern within the study region. This result may be expanded to a general conjecture that these are the areas which can be considered as entry points from where the Neolithic dwellers entered the Khasi and Jaintia hills (Figure 19).

Nature of Neolithic Finds

A large proportion of the findings in this research are based mainly on stone implements that have already, been exposed to the surface due to artificial disturbance like jhum cultivation or because of the natural erosion of the covering soil. The impact of the former condition is far more common in the area of field study since the practice of jhum cultivation still very common, especially in the Ri-Bhoi region where regeneration of vegetation is very fast owing to the fertility of the soil. At the site of Umiam-Barapani, there is evidence of the disturbance of the site caused by the recurring impact of the water pressure from the artificial lake which gradually exposed the embedded stone tools lying originally on hillocks close to the erstwhile Umiam stream. It is on the basis of archaeological evidence derived from such context that the level of profusion in the occurrences of stone tools has been tabulated in order to get some insights into the spread and concentration of the Neolithic sites around the study region.

Neolithic Finds and their Cultural Implications

Since the southern precipitous zones have not produced any form of Neolithic evidence, it is safe to presume at this juncture, that this zone locally known as the *War* region of the central Meghalaya plateau had not been able to attract the movement of people during the Neolithic period[41]. It is however, important to add in this context that a highly complex Megalithic tradition did flourish throughout this zone as evident from the vast array of monuments, a tradition that continues to survive to the present times. Since this zone lies close to the plains of Bangladesh, its importance was probably recognized only when trading activity between the hill dwellers and the plains started in the later period. This assumption is better attested on the fact that most of the so called ancient settlements from where the modern villages of this region traced their origin are generally located on the steep slopes close to the path which leads to the markets on the plains of Bangladesh. This observation allows us to speculate that the movement of the people into this precipitous zone of the Khasi hills was relatively later.

The concentration of Neolithic sites in the Ri-Bhoi region is shown by the fact that Neolithic implements are reported from almost all the existing villages in the region. The moist-humid climate, the numerous streams, the fertility of the land, the abundance of floral diversity and the surrounding hills on the sides are some of the most important features which have attracted Neolithic settlers in the region. The entire Ri-Bhoi low lands offer great opportunity for Neolithic men to exploit such diverse vegetation. The gemorphological condition of the region being characterised by very

---

[41] The *War* region specialized in the cultivation of betel nuts and other some horticultural crops. Large scale cultivation of food grains is not seen in this region.

undulating hills and fertile soil provided scope for *jhum* cultivators from the Neolithic period onwards. Ethnographic survey clearly shows that a high rate of *jhum* cultivation is still concentrated in the central Meghalaya plateau around the northern belt. As much of the stone implements collected from the region were recovered from the surface of the hill slopes or terraces of the hills, there is substantial evidence to indicate that, the hill slopes are areas of great attraction for the Neolithic farmers of the region (Plate 16). Ethnographic parallels fully supported the archaeological evidences as even to the present day *jhum* cultivators continue to exploit the hill slopes for cultivation.

For the sake of adding more information about the importance of Ri-Bhoi as a nuclear zone of Neolithic occupation, an oral tradition that has been preserve among the Bhoi khasis was recorded by Dr. Hamlet Bareh (Bareh, 1991, p.24);

The ancient khasis arrived into their present habitat from a coastal region through a long and arduous journey for a span of 12 years in search of good lands. The tradition further recounts that any of the first batches arrived here for colonizing would squeeze the best lands which they claimed ownership followed by other batches who laid hold on the other arable wet rice land. The process continued which made the last batches to transverse on and who were compelled to develop the terrace rice farming on low level lands or valleys or were pushed to some remote hills to develop dry rice cultivation. The last batches were pushed downwards to develop the horticultural fruit farming. It is further stated that they came to the hills carrying paddy seeds in seven boats during that journey (sic).

Turning towards the central upland zone to the sites of Umjajew, San Mer and Nongpyuir-Myrkhan of the Khasi hills, Neolithic evidence were recorded on a very large scale in terms of numbers and extent. However, except for the few finished tools, the entire collection from this zone is composed of cores, waste flakes and unfinished tools which are made mostly from amphibolites material. All these sites are found close to the source of the Umiam stream and therefore proved their direct affiliation with the

Umiam-Barapani site. The evidence also reflected a distinct pattern on the movement of Neolithic people who probably reached to the source of the Umiam stream on the south after following its course from the northeast. It is important to show that the site of Nongpyiur-Myrkhan which lies closest to the source of the Umiam stream reveal the highest percentage of cores and waste flake evidences throughout the entire area under-study. Even the evidence of iron slag is also recorded from this site. Although the association between the iron slag and the stone flakes cannot be conclusively drawn, a hypothesis can be forwarded at this stage, that the large scale use of iron may have taken place around this very area, and intensified further towards the southern upland zones. Such hypothesis is not improbable when we consider that the most of the villages north of Nongpyuir stretching right towards Sohra or Cherapunjee represent a massive belt iron smelting, the remnants of the industry which are still visible even to this day.

Looking towards the relatively much colder areas of west Khasi hills, Neolithic presence have so far been found from the sites of Nongspung and Wahlang which are located near the Nongspung or Langrei stream. The material and technology of the tools collected from the two sites of West Khasi hills bears the basic characteristic feature of the stone tools recorded from the Neolithic site of Upper-Shilong San Mer factory site. It can be seen that the two sites of West Khasi hills are a direct extension from the latter sites. As far as ethnographic sources are concerned, the concept of thunder axe is also familiar to some of the elderly people of these two villages who claimed sightings of such axes in the past (Plate 21) which may therefore allow us to speculate that more Neolithic sites could be present in this part of the Khasi hills if intensive survey is undertaken. Although the western part of this region shares its border with Garo hills, the morphological evidence of stone tools from these two sites showed no indication that the Neolithic tradition of the area arrived from the side of the Garo hills. In fact, it has to be again emphasise, that the stone tools from this part bear, a distinct signature of the Neolithic industry from the Khasi hills.

Evidence from the Khasi upland zone, which faced a relatively colder winter than the rest of the region under the study area, produced fewer evidences of finished tools compared to that of Ri-Bhoi region which perhaps shows that the uplands were not exploited in the same degree as that of the Ri-Bhoi during the Neolithic period. However the discovery of a factory site with large concentration of waste flakes and cores from upper Shillong-San-Mer, and Nongpyuir-Myrkhan 5 kilometers apart to south close to the source of the Umiam stream only suggest that the upland zone was also occupied by the Neolithic people on a large scale.

Hypotheses can be put forth to provide some explanation to the phenomenon and also to augment the absence of dating sources;

Firstly, the factory sites of the upland zone must have been utilized mainly for stone manufacturing as a factory site which probably worked to supply finished stone tools to distant places including the sites of west Khasi hills and Ri-Bhoi.

Secondly, Neolithic stone implements for jhum cultivation were used more abundantly in the Ri-Bhoi areas than the upland zone because of the fertility of the soil in this region. Thus the use of stone implements probably lasted much longer in the Ri-Bhoi than the upland zone. It is on the basis of this assumption that finished tools were recovered from almost all parts of Ri-Bhoi region but less from the upland zone. In further support of such hypothesis, the ethnographic survey shows that the present inhabitants of Ri-Bhoi are more acquainted with the concept of 'thunder axe' than the inhabitants of other parts of the area under study.

Thirdly, an assumption can be made that probably the upland zones were occupied much later that the Ri-Bhoi region, maybe around the transitional phase between that of the stone age and the time when iron had come into common use, a stage which be perhaps culturally

associated with the massive building of Megalithic monuments on the upland zone.

With regard to Jaintia hills only those areas which are close to the Cachar hills and Ri-Bhoi region have been able to produce Neolithic evidences, the major parts of Jaintia hills is devoid of any trace of Neolithic implements. Evidence of Megalithic complex, consisting large square stone cist, menhirs and dolmens and stone circles (Plate 17) along with large debris of iron slag was however recorded from the village of Sutnga which has traditionally been known as the seat of one the earliest headquarter of a chiefdom society in Jaintia hills (Lyngdoh, 1964, pp.8-80). The villagers in around this village claimed that the stone tools were also seen around the site of the Megalithic complex (which survived till today), but in recent past, a local healer took them all away for making medicine. But from within the same geographical space, there are reports of frequent discovery of stone tools by cultivators from the jhum fields which lies north of the village of Sutnga that are still under the covering of dense forest. Thus even without any physical verification of the stone tools, there is reasonable ground to conclude, that the Neolithic culture along the Jaintia hills extended till the areas close to the village of Sutnga. It may be further speculated, that the cultural and political importance of Sutnga village documented in traditional sources could have date back to the Neolithic or late Neolithic phase, a case similar with the sites of the Khasi uplands. On the other hand, the evidences, of large concentration of iron slag spreading throughout the village of Trang Blang in the *War*-Jaintia of southern Jaintia hills points to the fact that these areas were occupied only when iron had come into use, as no report of stone tools was ever heard of from the people of the villages around this area. Similar to the condition of the southern slopes of the *War* areas of Khasi hills, the War Jaintia areas of the southern parts Jaintia hills also gained attraction only after trading activity with the plains of Bangladesh started.

In further support of the above hypothesis, ethnographic survey conducted during the course of this research shows that the local people inhabiting the upland zones are less acquainted with the concept of *U Sdie Pyrthat* or the Thunder Axe, the local name used by the khasis for the Neolithic stone axe (See Chapter on Ethnoarcheology) whereas the similar survey from the lowland zones of Ri-Bhoi an parts of Jaintia hills reveal the opposite result. Most of the elderly people have heard about *U Sdie Pyrthat* and have come across sightings of thunder axe at some point time during their lifetime.

The data recovered so far, clearly shows that, the upland zones in the interior parts of the Khasi and Jaintia hills were occupied much later in the Neolithic times, and further evidence seems to indicate that the Neolithic settlers of the these upland zones were probably the forerunner of the people who developed the iron technology and authored the Megalithic tradition.

The Neolithic sites of the Khasi and Jantia hills are evenly distributed along the outline of the eastern portion of the Jaintia hills as indicated by the evidence from the sites around Shiliang Myntang-Chei Bnai and the northern portion of the Khasi hills along the entire region close to the Karbi Anglong district, where the excavated sites of Marakdola and Sarutaru are located.

Till new evidence surface up, it can be safely concluded that the Neolithic elements of the Khasi and Jaintia hills are the direct offshoot of the outliner Neolithic from the Cachar hills and the Karbi Anglong region which are probably the very areas from where the Neolithic elements could have entered the Khasi and Jaintia hills. Nothing can be said about the relationship between the Neolithic elements of the area under study and those of Garo hills until more evidence surfaces from the side of the west khasi hills. But it is almost certain that the Neolithic element of Garo hills must have used the same route along the lower Brahmaputra valley in their east west migration movement

Factors Influencing Intra-Hills Movement of the Neolithic People

With regard to the factors which have generated the pattern of movement of the Neolithic people within and around the area of the study region, the cycle of Jhum cultivation is one of the most decisive factors. Another hypothesis may be forwarded that the Neolithic farmers that the Neolithic farmers who arrived into the Khasi hills appeared to have come from the Cachar hills and took a westward turn (Figure 19). Probably in the initial phase they were concentrated around the periphery of the Ri-Bhoi region and the northern parts of the Jaintia hills. Those who exploited the hill tracts of the Ri-Bhoi region followed the southern course of the Umiam and Umkhen river and one group reached the site of Umiam-Barapani from where they began to make their venture into the heart land of the Khasi hills on the upland zones of the plateau.

As far as the West Khasi hills are concerned, there is very little evidence to provide any form of understanding about the movement pattern of the people. Not a single site was discovered from the western side of the Umiam gorge opposite to the sites of Upper Shillong and the rest of the sites locating in the Khasi upland. It is however most likely, that the Neolithic element from the Ri-Bhoi especially from the site of Umiam-Barapani took a westerly direction and moved along the foot hills of *U Lumdiengiei* and reached the areas close to the Khri River in the West Khasi hills. This is well attested through the claims made by the people from the village of Nongum in West Khasi hills which is located close to the Khri river (Fig. 13) about the sightings of Neolithic tools in the past.

The climate and fertility soil is another possible influencing factor that affected the migration pattern. The heavy rainfall and colder climate of the upland zones of the Khasi hills and Jaintia hills are not so favourable for the Neolithic settlers which therefore seems to explain the reason as to why the distribution of the Neolithic sites in the region are sparse compared to the moist-humid climate region of the Ri-Bhoi valley .

With regard to the Khasi hills, the Umiam river appeared to be the route for the movement of the people as they followed it upstream towards its source in the Khasi upland. Whatever trace of the Neolithic evidence so far discovered in the Khasi Hills are found between the Umiam and Umkhen rivers which meets in the border of Karbi Anglong district of Assam in Ri-Bhoi district. And the Neolithic site of Umiam-Barapani appear to be the terminal end of Neolithic population since it is the biggest site in the entire area under study. The Neolithic people moved from the Umiam-Barapani site upstream towards the north east where surface collections of Neolithic implements were recovered at regular interval. The Umiam stream played an important role on the Neolithic culture not only in the Khasi hills, but throughout its entire northern Ri-Bhoi region. Among the people of the Ri-Bhoi region, there is a traditional story which narrates of a racing competition between the Umiam and Umsiang (a stream which rises from Raitong village in Ri-Bhoi) as they surged to reach their confluence at Umtrai close to the Karbi Anglong district. This tradition allows scope to expand upon the archaeological evidences. The importance of these two streams in shaping the history and culture of the people in the region under study right from the very incipient stage of their culture, going back to the period of beginning of the Neolithic phase in this region.

The presence of the massive stone making factory at the sites of Umiam-Barapani, Upper Shillong, Umjajew and Nongpyuir-Myrkhan seems to point out that these Neolithic factory sites in the Khasi uplands along the Umiam stream have evolved as specialized factory sites that probably supplies finished tools for agricultural use and exploitation of the rich soil of Ri-Bhoi region. In the context of this assumption, the Ri-Bhoi region, must have supported the stable Neolithic population of the region and continued to remain still the granary of the people of these hills, while on the other hand the Khasi uplands evolved as an area specialized in stone tool production or industrial sites, a process which continued till iron had come into common use. The upland became the centre of all economic activities. The

evidence of great Megalithic building in the upland zone largely reflect the stability of the society supported by a strong economic base which gradually crystallized into the Shillong chiefdom.

On Neolithic-Megalithic transition in the region under-study

Evidence from the upland sites of upper Shillong, Nongpyiur-Myrkhan, reveal a clear case of transition between the Neolithic and the Megalithic. From the site of Upper Shillong-San Mer, an apparent transition is found when cores and waste flakes are found within 5-10 cm below the surface on a hillock where four rows of Megalithic monuments in the form menhirs and dolmens clusters. The discovery of this site offers an additional opportunity to understand the choice of selecting a space for erection of Megalithic monuments. In the context of this site, the same mound was used for manufacturing stone tools at some point of time, and later on chosen as a place for erecting rows of megalithic monuments. There is very little evidence to support an assumption that these archaeological objects have been artificially brought into this place even with the fact that they have been definitely displaced from their actual context due to the use of this land for cultivation in the recent past. At the level of this research nothing can be said about the relationship between the two archaeological contexts, but one point is clear enough that, this site calls for a more complex study as it can help to expand our understanding into the megalithic tradition in these hills especially in the context of space selection for erecting memorial monuments. In the same way the site is also important in providing information about the continuity and transition of Neolithic elements at the stage when Megalithic tradition have already made their appearance in these hills.

Since the areas surrounding the factory site of upper Shillong shows large concentration of Megalithic monuments, there is ample scope to speculate that this area was probably occupied during the Neolithic period and the occupation continues into the Megalithic phase. Traditional history further supports the archaeological data, and strengthens the argument on the process of continuity of settlement right to the period when social and political formation began to take shape on the Khasi hills, as describe in traditional history of this area (Lyngdoh, 1962, pp. 81-102).

In further support of the above hypothesis, the Khasi uplands on the whole are flooded with Megalithic monuments and the above reports of colonial workers also supplied us with valuable information about the large scale iron smelting that flourished on the upland zones yet none of them made any reference of such a smelting process going on in the Ri-Bhoi areas or the low land zone. These records partially suggest some form of a cultural demarcation which can be associated with the Khasi uplands for which the zone probably represents the stage of transition in the Neolithic-Megalithic cultures in the region. The discovery of the already mentioned Neolithic factory site at Upper Shillong underneath the Megalithic surface is one such archaeological evidence which strongly support this hypothesis. Oral history claimed that the Megalithic monuments which spread around Upper Shillong are linked to the folks who established the first chiefdom society of the region popularly referred to as the *Hima Shillong* or the Shillong Chiefdom. Thus the Neolithic site of upper Shillong which revealed evidences of occupation from the stone age right to the chiefdom society identified archeologically with the Megalithic monuments represents a clear case of cultural continuity of Neolithic and Megalithic culture in this zone.

As similar type of evidence also comes from the Neolithic site of Sohpet Bneng which lies close to the upland belt near the Umiam-Brarpani site. From the site, Neolithic stone implements were collected from an area where large numbers of Megalithic monuments were also found. Oral history recorded, that, the authors of the Megalithic complex from the site of Sohpet Bneng are associated with the inhabitants of the ancient provincial capital of a chiefdom called *Mawbuh*. Thus, this is another evidence regarding the Neolithic-Megalithic cultural continuity in the region.

Transition to Iron Age

On the evidence of intensity of stone tool occurrence, a pattern has already emerged from the present study which has helped to offer some clue about the movement of the Neolithic folks within this micro-environmental niche. This evidence points that the Khasi uplands in central part of the study region was being occupied much less in terms of the land coverage compared to the Northern belt of the Ri-Bhoi region. There is also a general pattern in the process of movement of the Neolithic folks, showing more of North to South and North to East movement which hence offers additional support to the hypothesis of Ri-Bhoi region being the area of attraction for the Neolithic people. The concentration of Neolithic evidences showed a distinct pattern that from the Ri-Bhoi to the Khasi upland zone, all the sites are found along the course of the Umiam stream and reaching its source the Neolithic population expanded and moved towards west Khasi hills as evident from the archaeological findings from the sites of Nongspung and Wahlang. From the two Neolithic sites of Nongpyuir-Myrkhan, which are located very close to the source of the Umiam river, traces of Iron slag are found in large deposits scattered over a vast area. Such evidence are found throughout the upland zones which thereby opens up further scope of speculating that the upland zones had attracted the Neolithic folks who followed the course of the Umiam river and eventually mastered the iron technology and carried it throughout the upland areas.

There are oral-narratives which are preserved in the Khasis tradition regarding the role of iron and its impact on the process of migration. Although lacking in details, regarding the source of the tradition, it is still interesting to quote Dr. Hamlet Bareh who recounts one such tradition from the Bhoi region. He wrote that,

"the Khasi tradition pin-points that the first Khasis reached their present terrain for searches of metals, iron pyrites and rocks which catered with their economic and cultural needs (sic) (Bareh, 1991, p.25).

Another scholar also speculated that the search for iron was one factor which moved the people from Jaintia hills (may mean areas close to Ri-Bhoi) into the upland zones. To quote, the scholar observes:

It was in part of the search and location of Iron ore that the Khasis moved from the first settlements in the Jaintia Hills (Syiemlieh, 1994, p. 42).

Evidence of the traditional iron industry was recorded by the colonial workers in its dying stage but, has nevertheless helped to provide ample evidence about the extent of this industry in the hills (Oldham, 1854. pp.70-77). Gurdon, who had written comprehensively about the Khasis observed;
"The Iron Industry in the former days was an important one. Evidence of this can be seen at Nongkrem and Laitlyngkot in the shape of large granite boulders which have fallen on the ground owing to the softer rocks which filled the interstices between the boulders having been worked out by the iron workers, their process being to dig out the softer ferruginious rock and then extract the iron ore from it by means of washing (Gurdon, 1914, p.57).

Writing much earlier, Yule further wrote;
"..the ore is (with exception) not smelted in the villages adjoining, which it is procured. It is sold in Baskets...carried for many miles to the village where the smelting furnace is located...In most cases the crude iron is again carried to other villages when it is manufactured and set (Yule, 1842, pp. 853-857).

The iron was once the chief industry of the Khasi hills and a considerable quantity of this metal used to be exported into the plains of Bangladesh through Sylhet. Although recorded during its dying stage, till 1858, the annual export of pig iron was estimated to be 45,000 *maunds* valued to about Rs. 67,500/- during those days[42]. The figures certainly helped to evaluate the role of iron as a base of the economy of the people. Thomas Oldham, provided a detailed report on the process of manufacturing iron. He stated that, there is a complete division of labour after the stage when pig iron was finished into working implements

in the hills itself to the extent that different villages have specialised in the manufacturing of selected implements. Further points of interest in his report, was that, fuel used for the entire process was charcoal (Oldham, 1854, pp. 72-74). Estimating the amount of iron production from the reports, the demand for charcoal must have led to a large scale deforestation of the upland zones and probably reshaped much of the original forest and vegetation pattern of the hills; the replacement of broad leaf vegetation to conifer vegetation was perhaps one such consequence[43].

Neolithic and Iron Technology and State Formation in Khasi and Jaintia hills

The Neolithic sites that are found all along the Khasi-Jaintia hills were recovered mostly from areas which later on developed into strong seat of political power. There is a strong indication on the continuity of occupation of these sites right from the Neolithic to the later stage as supported by the evidence of Megalithic structures and traces of iron slag.

The following sites reveal this continuity;

The site of Upper Shillong-San Mer
Traces of stone artifacts in massive numbers in their unfinished stage, Megalithic structures spread over a wide area and evidence of iron working found around its vicinity. Oral history established that this area was the earliest seat of chiefdom society in the area under study.

---

[43] In support of such an argument, it is important to note that the Sacred Grooves or the 'traditional reserved forest' are mostly found in the Khasi uplands and this was a practiced that deates back to a remote period. In the Khasi traditional belief, there is so much of taboo attached with the Sacred Grooves that who ever cutted down a tree from these forest would faced the wrath of the forest's presiding deity and will suffer physical deformity. It is also interesting to point out that such sacred grooves are actually compose of only Broad-Leaf vegetation, a sharp contrast to the conifer vegetation type (pine Forest) that covers the present landscape. Human agency may have therefore played a decisive role in the replacement of the original forest and in the context of this argument, this would be closely linked to deforestatation owing to the demand of charcoal which is the basic requirement in Iron Smelting. Thus it can be hypothesised that the degree of human exploitation in contrary generated the concept of preservation of such forest (Original type).

---

[42]A maund is equivalent to 40 Kgs.

The Site of Sohpet Bneng

Traces of Neolithic habitation on the basis of finished stone tools, Megalithic monuments, Cremation platform and iron slag evidences have also surfaced out from this site. Oral history associated this site as once a provincial headquarter of a large Chiefdom which exists till today. On the basis of folk lore, this is certainly ancestral site.

Site of Nongspung

Traces of Neolithic tools regularly reported by the people from their fields, Megalithic monuments and massive traces of iron working. Oral history describes this area as the headquarters of the earliest chiefdom of West Khasi hills which exist till today.

Site of Sutnga

Stone tools although not collected, yet, have been reported regularly by the people from the fields and there are traces of large number of Megalithic structures and iron working evidences. Oral history as well as written history, suggest that this is the first headquarters of the earliest chiefdom of Jaintia hills.

The few sites mentioned above are clear evidence of the continuous occupation of the sites which later developed as seats of some of the earliest chiefdoms that emerged in the Khasi and Jaintia hills. State formation in the area under study began in the very areas, which also reveal strong evidence of occupation right from the Neolithic period. This certainly point to the fact that the Neolithic implements in the hills have played a major role in supporting the stable economy of their respective area thereby provided a strong platform for the emergence of a well established chiefdom society. The above evidence also provided enough reasons to speculate that the Neolithic users in the area under study continued to experiment with iron technology and also authored the Megalithic culture in the hills.

A final hypothesis may be forwarded here to establish a direct relationship between the Neolithic folks and the authors of iron technology in the hills and to associate the Megalithic culture with the Neolithic sites. This research has come up with serious evidence to prove that the present inhabitants of the Khasi and Jaintia hills are the direct descendants of the Neolithic folks who had entered the region with Neolithic technology. It is however not clear whether they arrived at these hills already with some knowledge of iron technology or not, but on the basis of recurrence of evidence it is certain that, they were the same people who began the use of iron in these hills and later on master the art till it flourished into a major industry and probably became the backbone of the socio-economic system of the people till the 19th century before the colonial power finally apprehended its growth.

++

PLATES

Cist: Bone Repository

Standing Stone with Dolmed infront

Stone Circles

Plate 1: Megalithic Monuments of Khasi-Jaintia Hills, Meghalaya

Tree Stumps

Tree Stumps

Upper portion of surviving tree

Plate 2: Remains of the Broad Leaf Forest, Umiam-Barapani, Ri-Bhoi Dist.

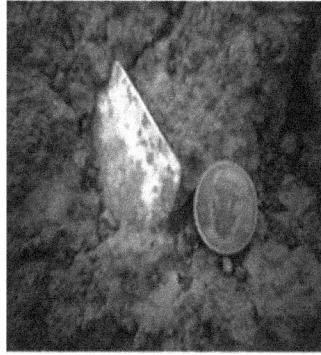

Plate 3: In-Situ tools at Umiam-Barapani, Ri-Bhoi Dist.

Tools from Mawrong

Tools from Sohpet Bneng

Plate 4: Tools from Ri-Bhoi Dist.

Unfinished Tools from San-Mer (Upper Shillong)

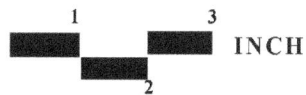

1　　　3
INCH
2

Unfinished Tools from Umjajew

Plate 5: Unfinished Tools from East Khasi Hills Dist.

95

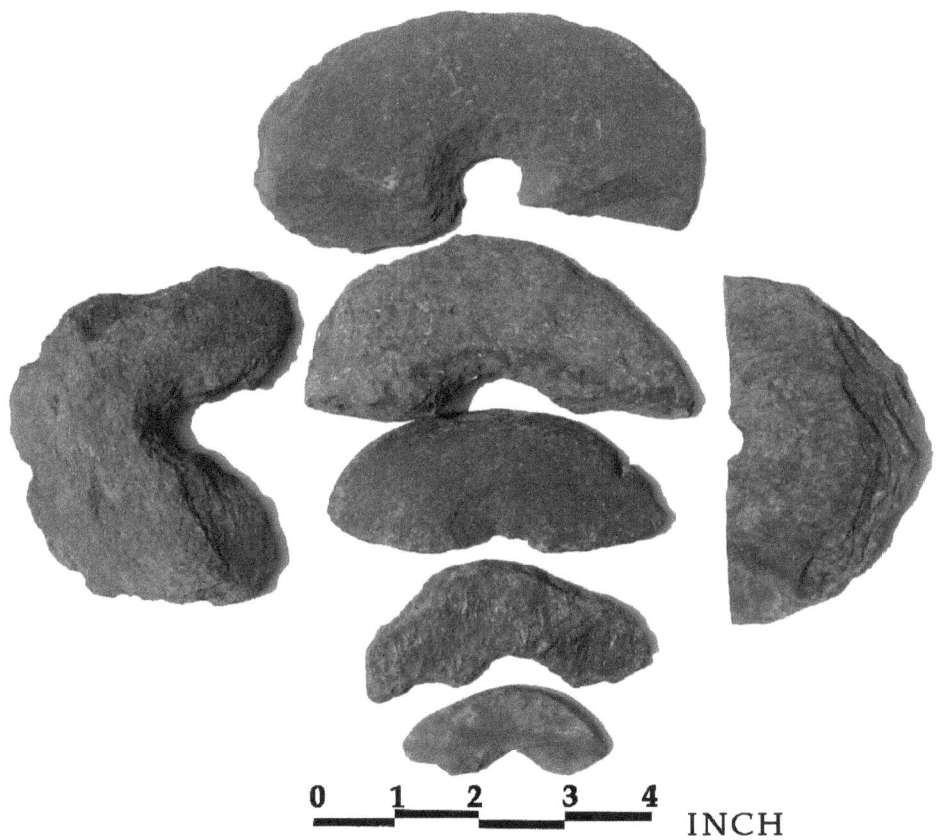

Plate 6: Ring Stones from Umiam-Barapani, Ri-Bhoi Dist.

Potsherds from Neolithic Sopet-Bneng, Ri-Bhoi Dist.
Cord impressed potsherds are seen on right side and quartz materials
are seen on the surface of potsherds.

Cord-impressed potsherds from Umiam-Barapani, Ri-Bhoi Dist.

Potsherds from San-Mer (Upper Shillong), East Khasi Hills Dist.

Plate 7: Potsherds from Sopet-Bneng, Umiam-Barapani & San-Mer

97

Plate 8: In-Situ Wheel Made Potteries, Umiam-Barapani, Ri-Bhoi Dist.

Tools from Mawbri, Ri-Bhoi Dist.

Tools from the sire near Khanduli, Jaintia Hills Dist.

Plate 9: Tools from Mawbri & Khanduli

99

No.1

0   1   2   INCH

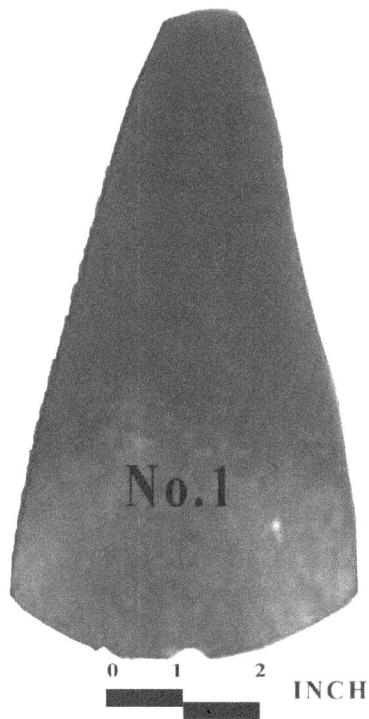

A polished axe owned by a villager in Khliehumtem village, Ri-Bhoi Dist.

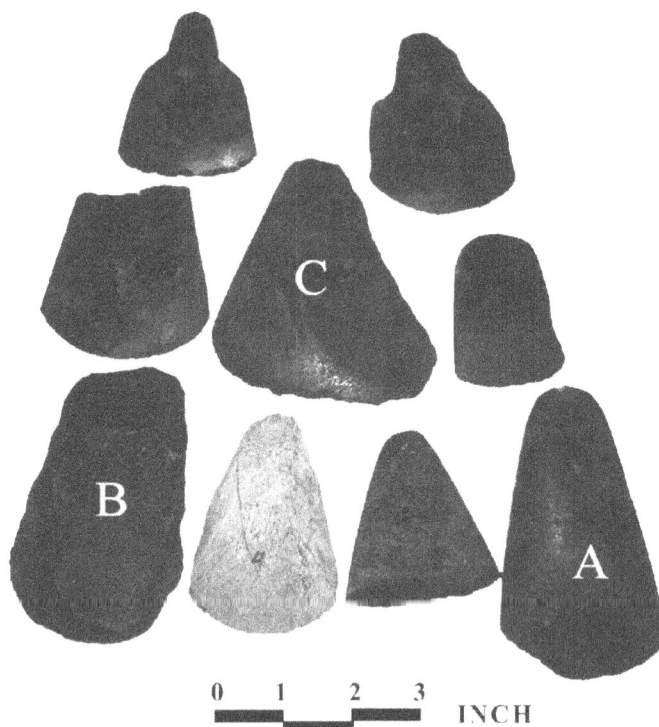

C

B   A

0   1   2   3   INCH

Tools from Iapngar Areas, Ri_Bhoi Dist.

Plate 10: Polished Axe from a villager of Ri-Bhoi Dist. & Tools from Iapngar

100

Tools from the site of Umjajew, East Khasi Hills Dist.

A finished tool from San-Mer (upper Shillong)

A finished tool from Tynring
Plate 11: Tools from Umjajew, San-Mer & Tynrlng

101

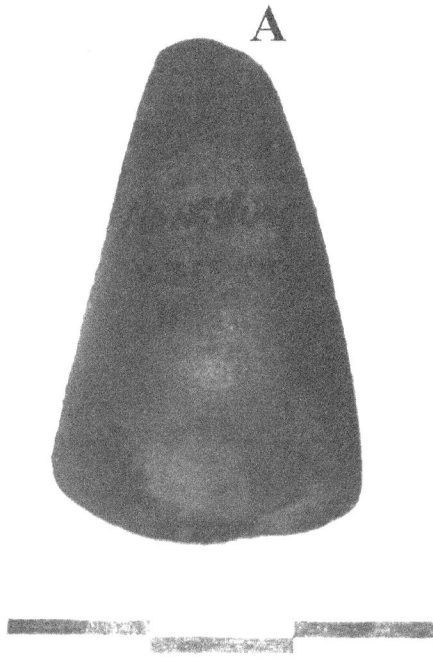

From Nongspung village

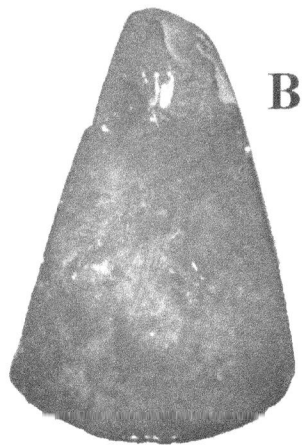

From Waklang village

Plate 12: Tools from West Khasi Hills

102

A

Megalithic Monumnets at San-Mer (Upper Shillong);
A Neolithic Factory site lies underneath

B

Trial digging at the factory site San-Mer
Note: Approximate depth of the crow bar is 3 feet
Circle shows the cores and flake evidences

Plate 13: Megalithic at San-Mer

1

INCH

A tool from Nongkhram

2

0   1   2   3

Tools from Umbi, Tyrso, Umswai and Amjong

Plate 14: Tools from Nongkhram, Umbi, Tyrso, Umswai & Amjong

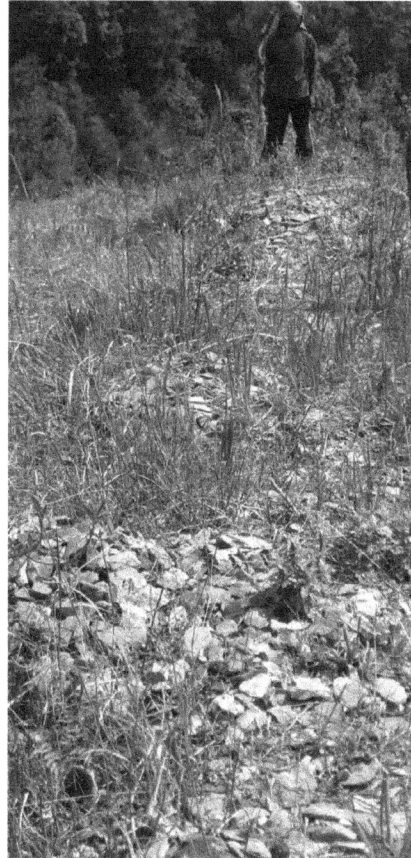

Plate 15: Flakes/Cores from Myrkhan

105

A

Hill slope like this was exploited by jhum cultivators of Neolithic period, Umiam Stream

B

RED ARROWS INDICATES AREAS FROM WHERE TOOLS ARE COLECTED

The site of Umiam-Barapani

Plate 16: Hill Slopes Conducive for Jhum Cultivation

Remains of Megalithic Monuments

One among the many stone circles in the same area

Plate 17: Megalithic Site of Sutnga

D

INCH
1   2   3

Srapper/Harvester

A

1   2   3   4   INCH
CM
1   3   5   7

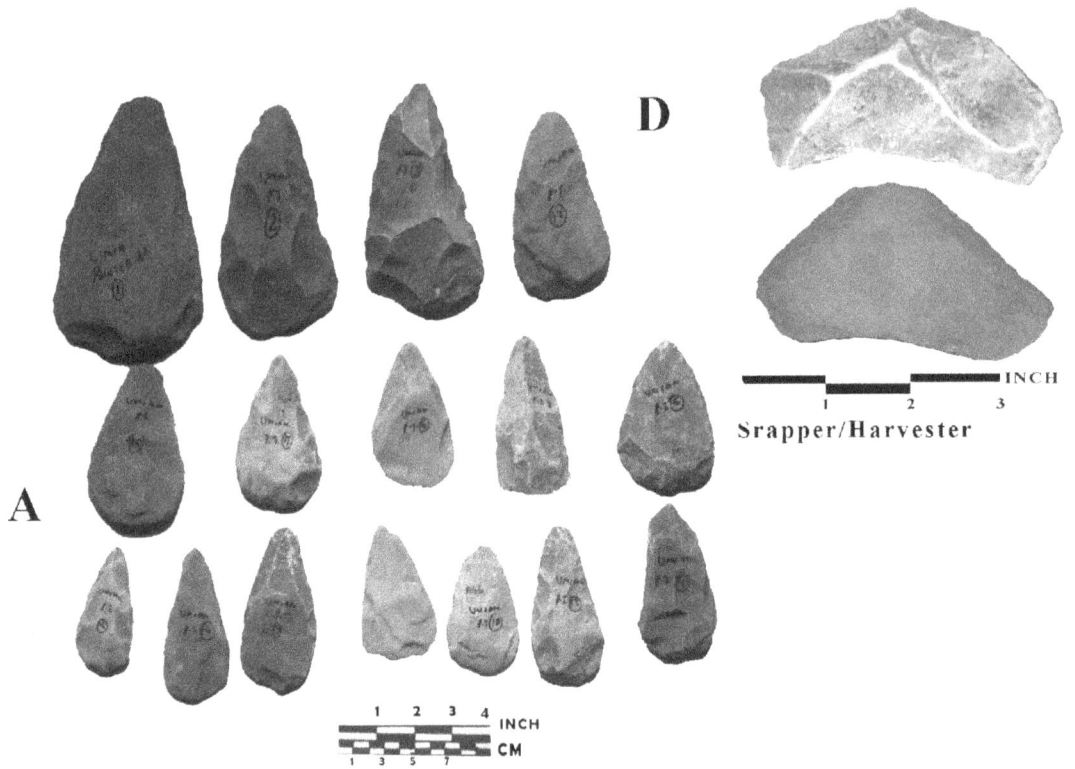

Pointed Butt Unfinished (unground) Tools from Umiam-Barapani

B

1   2
CM

C

INCH
CM

Round Butt Unfinished (unground) Tools from Barapani   Unfinished Shouldered/Tanged

Plate 18: Unfinished and Scrapper/Harvester Tools from Study Area

108

A

Round Butt Types of Tools

B

Pointed-Butt Axes

C

Chisel and Adze

Plate 19: Round & Pointed Butt Tools and Chiesel & Adzes from Study Area

109

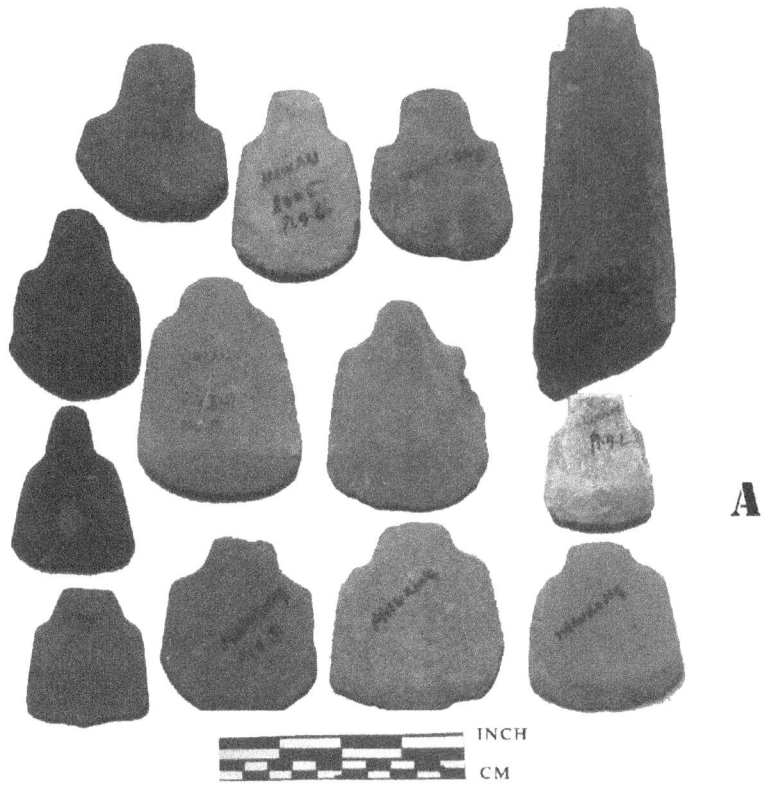

Shouldered Tools

Tanged Types Tools

Plate 20: Shouldered and Tanged Tools from Study Area

110

Mr. Kodri Syiemlieh, Nongspung village (West Khasi Hills)

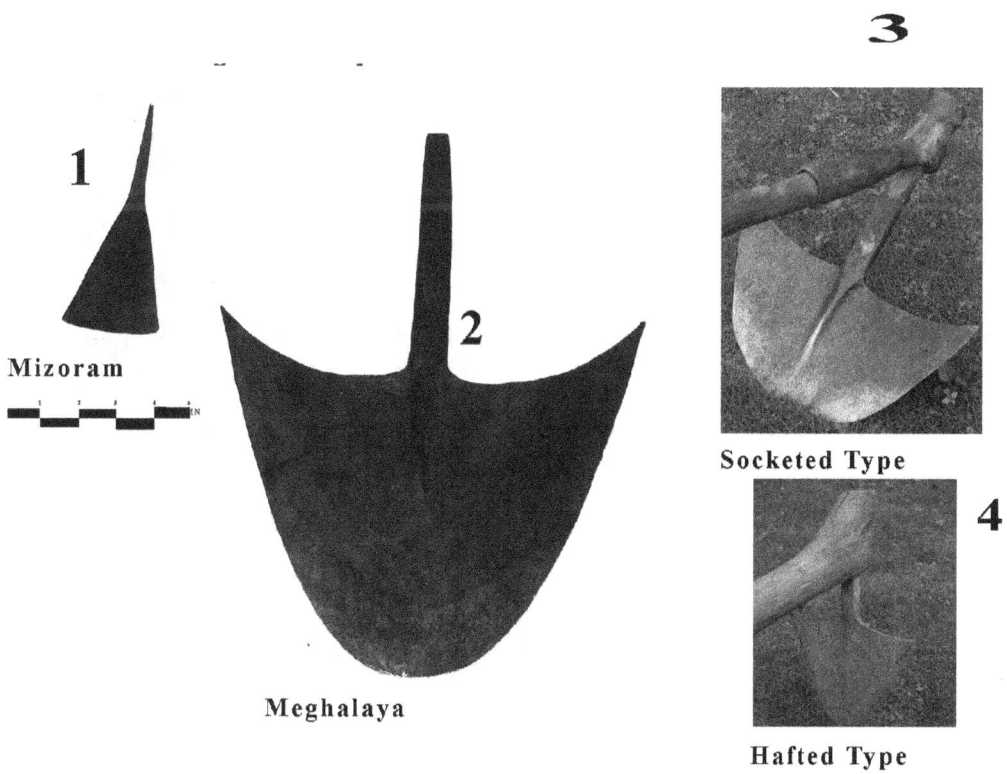

1

Mizoram

2

Meghalaya

3

Socketed Type

4

Hafted Type

Plate 21: Axe and Hoes

111

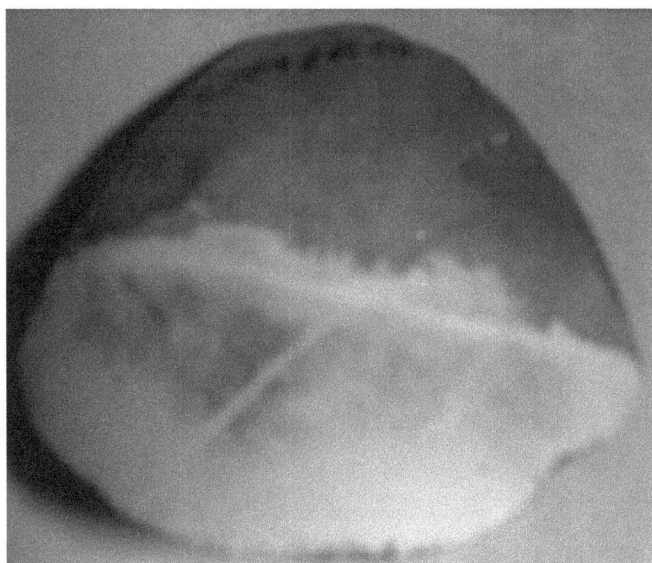

0   **1` ` ` ` ` ` ` ` `2 INCH`**

Patina on Polish Tool

0   **1`INCH**

Patina on Unfinished Tool

Plate 22: Patina on Stone Implements

REFERENCES

Allchin Bridget and Raymond Allchin. 1989. *The Rise of Civilization in India and Pakistan.*Delhi.

Ansari, Z.D. et.al. 1970. Excavations at Ambari (Gauhati):1970. *Journal of University of Poona, Humanities* Section, No.35, pp.79-87.

Ascher Robert. 1961. Analogy in Archaeological Interpretation. *South West Journal of Anthropology,* Volume 17, pp.317-321.

Austin-Godwin, H.H. 1872. On the stone monuments of the Khasi hill tribes and on some of the peculiar rites and customs of the people. *Journal of Anthropological Institute of Great Britain and Ireland.* I, pp.122-143.

—— 1875. A Celt found at th Khasi Hills Shillong. *Proceedings of the Asiatic Society of Bengal,* p.158.

Balfour, H. 1929. Concerning Thunderbolts. *Folk-Lore.* pp. 37-49.

Bareh Hamlet. 1991. *The Art History of Meghalaya.* Delhi.

Brum Adam et.al. 2007. Stone Axe Technology in Neolithic South India:New Evidence from the Sanganakallu-Kupgal Region, Mideastern Karnataka. *Asian Perspectives,* 46(1) pp.65-95.

1967. *The History and Culture of the Khasi People.* Guwahati.

Barron Lt. 1872. Note on stone Implements from the Naga Hills. *Journal of anthropological Institute of Great Britain and Ireland.* 1, pp. 62-63.

Bhuyan, G. N. 1993. Archaeology in North-East India. In Dilip Medhi (ed) *Man and Environment in North East India,* (1) New Delhi, p. 34-35.

Brown Coggin. 1917. *Catalogue of Prehistoric Antiquities in Indian Museum.* Calcutta.

Chang, K.C. 1967. Major aspects of Interrelationship of Archaeology and Ethnology. *Current Anthropology,* 8 (3), pp. 227-235.

Childe Gordon V.G. 1936. *Man Makes Himself.* London.

Chowdhury, J.N. 1996. *Ki Khun Khasi Khara (The Khasi People.* Shillong.

Choudhuri P. C. 1966. *The History of the civilization of the people of Assam to the 12th century.*Gauhati.

Clark, G.D. 1969. *World Prehistory, A New Outline.* Cambridge

Clarke Hyde. 1877. On Prehistoric Names and Weapons. *Journal of anthropological Institute of Great Britain and Ireland.* 6, pp.142-149.

Cockburn, G. 1879. Notes on stone Implements, Khasi hills etc. *Journal of Asiatic Society of Bengal,* part I (48), pp. 133-143.

Cushing Frankl. 1886. A study of Pueblo Pottery as illustrative of Zuni culture growth. B*ureau of American Ethnology Fourth Annual Report.*Washington D.C.,pp. 467-521.

Dair Verma A.K. 1988. *Neolithic culture of Eastern India.* Delhi.

Dalton, E.T. 1872. *Descriptive Ethnology of Bengal.* Calcutta.

Dani A.H. 1960. *Pre and Proto-History of Eastern India.* Calcutta.

Dinacauze F. Dina 2000. *Environmental Archaeology, Pinciples and Pactices.* Cambridge.

Davalikar, M.K. 1972. Archaeology of Gauhati. *Bulletin of Deccan College Research Institute,* 32(II), pp. 137-149.

David Nicholas. 1992. Integrating Ethnoarcheology: A Subtle Realist Perspective. *Journal of Anthropological Archeology.* 11, pp 330-359.

Donnan,C.B. et.al.(eds.) 1974. *Ethnoarcheology.* Institute of Archaeology Monograph. University of California, pp. 29-48.

Driem Van George. 1998. Neolithic correlates of ancient Tibeto-Burman migrations in Roger Bleech, et.al.(eds). *Archaeology and Language II. Archaeological data and Linguistic Hypotheses.* ONE WORLD ARCHEOLOGY. Routledge, London, pp. 67-114.

Eliade Mircea. 1996. The Reality of the Sacred. in Daniel Pals (ed), *Seven Theories of Religion.* Oxford University Press, pp. 158-197.

Gorman Chestor. 1971. The Hoabinhian and After: Subsistence pattern in Southeast Asia during the late Pleistocene and Early Recent Times. *World Archaeology.* 2(3), pp. 300-320.

Goswami, M.C. et.al. 1959. A Preliminary Report On Collection Of Neolithic Tool Types From Western Assam. *Man in India.* 39(1), pp. 312-324.

Gould R.A. 1968. Living Archeology.The Nataraja of Western Australia. *South western Journal of Anthropology.* 24, pp. 101-122.

Gupta Chandra Das Hem. 1993 On two shouldered Implements from Assam. *Journal of Asiatic Society of Bengal.* IX, pp. 291-93.

Gurdon, T.R.P. 1914. *The Khaisis.* London.

Jewkes Jesse. 1900. Tusayan migration tradition. *Bureau of American Ethnology, Annual Report,* No.19, pp. 577-633.

Habib Ifran. 2001. *Prehistory.* Aligarh Historian Society.

Haimendorf Furer Von. 1943. Megalithic Rituals among the Gadabas and Bondos of Orissa. *Journal of Asiatic Society of Bengal.* 9,(letters 4), p. 173.

Harris. D.(ed). 1996. *The Origins and the spread of agriculture and pastoralism in Eurasia.*London University.

Hingham, C.F.W. 1972 Intial model formulation in *terra incognita. In* David L Clarke (ed) *Models in Archeology,* London p. 451-464.

Hodder Ian. 1996. *The Domestication of Europe.* Blackwell, London.

—— 1983. Contextual Archaeology: an interpretation of Catal Huyuk and a discussion of agriculture. *Bulletin of the Institute of Archaeology.* pp. 43-56.

Hunter, W.W., *Statistical Account of Assam,* 1879, (Reprint, 1975).

Hussain Zahid 1996. Significant characteristics of a Neolithic site at Barapani (Khasi Hills). *North East India Historical Asociation.* 17th Session, pp. 111-118

Hutton J.H. 1928. Prehistory of Assam. *Man in India.* VIII, pp. 228-29.

Iyer Krishna L.A. 1967. *Kerela Megaliths and their Builders,* University of Madras .

Kent Susan, (ed). 1987. *Methods and Theory for activity area research; an ethnoarchaeological approach.* Columbia University Press. pp. 1-62.

Kleindienst Maxime, et.al. 1956. Living Action Archaeology: The Archaeological Inventory of Living Community. *Anthropology Tomorrow* 5 (1), pp. 75-78.

Vikrant Kumar et.al. 2008. Y-chromosome evidence suggests a common paternal heritage of Austro-Asiatic populations. *@http://www.biomedcentral.com,* BMC Evolutionary Biology. 7.

Layton Robert. 1999. Folklore and world view. *In Archeology and Folklore,* (eds) Amy Gazin Schwartz and Cornelius Holtorf. Routledge, London. pp.26-34.

Lyngdoh Pristilla. 1998. *Festival of the Khasi.*Shillong.

Lubbock John. 1867. The Stone tools of Upper Assam *Athenaeum* No. 2069. London, p. 822.

Mawlong Cecile. 2005. Dating the Northeastern Neolithic Cultures: Problems and Prospects. *North Eastern India Historical Association.* 25th Session.

___ 2007. The Making of the Khasi Identity. *International Seminar on Identity, Emotion and Culture: Language Literature of the sub-continent, circa 1900-1971.* Organised by ICHR, New Delhi and NEHU Shillong .

Mills J.P. and Hutton J.H. 1929. Ancient Monoliths of North Cachar. *Journal of Asiatic Society of Bengal.* XXV, pp. 295-298.

Medhi Dilip. (ed). 1993. *Man and Environment in North East India.* 1.New Delhi.

—— 1990. Prehistory of Assam. *Asian Perspective.* XXIX (1), pp. 37-44.

—— 2002. Archaeological Research in Karbi Anglong, Assam. *Man and Environment.* II, pp. 48-65.

Michlovic M.G. 1990. Folk archaeology in anthropological perspective. *Current Anthropology.*31, pp. 103-107.

Mitri Marco. 1998. *Living Megalithism of the Khasis: Special Reference to Umniuh-Tmar Village of the War Region.* Unpublished M.A. Dissertation. Deccan College, Pune.

——2005. An Ethnoarchaeological Study on the Folktale of U Lum SohpetBneng. *North Eastern India Historical Association.* 25th Session. pp. 65-71.

—— 2006. Report on the Neolithic tools from Sohpet Bneng Hill of Ri-Bhoi District in Meghalaya (An Ethno-archaeological Study. *North Eastern India Historical Association.* 26th Session, pp. 87-95.

___2008. Tradition and Archeology: The concept of Thunder Axe and evidences from North East India. *Nagaland University Research Journal.* pp. 17-27.

Momin Mignonette. (eds).2004. *Society and Economy in North East India.* (1). Delhi.

Narasimhaiah B. 1980. *Neolithic and Megalithic Cultures in Tamil Nadu.* Delhi.

Neinu, V. 1974. Recent Prehistoric Discoveries in Nagaland: A Survey. *Highlander,* Research Bulletin of the Department of Arts and Culture. Government of Nagaland. (2), pp. 5-7.

Neustupny Evzen. 1993. *Archaeological method.* Cambridge University Press.

Nicholas David, et.al. 2001. *Ethnoarchaeology in Action.* Cambridge.

Oldham Thomas. 1917. *On The Geological structure of a portion of Khasi Hills.* Bengal.

114

Oswalt W.H. 1974. Ethnoarcheology. In C.B. Donnan & C.W.Clewlow (eds). *Ethnoarcheology.* Institute of Archeology Monograph, University of California. pp. 3-14.

Pemberton, R.B. 1835. *Reports on the eastern frontier of British India.* Calcutta.

Paddayya. K. 1990. The New Archaeology and Aftermath. Pune.

Rao S.N. 1977. Excavations at Sarataru: A Neolithic site in Assam. *Man and Environment.* 1, pp. 39-43.

——1977. Continuity and Survival of Neolithic Traditions in Northeastern India. *Asian Perspectives,* XX(2), pp. 91-205.

Renfrew Collin and Bahn Paul. 1991. *Archeology, Theories Methods and Practices.* London.

T. Raychodhury. 1935. *Journal of Department of Letters.* xxvi, Calcutta University, p.1.

David Roy. 1936. Principles of Khasi Culture. *Folklore.* 47(4), pp. 375-393

Sankalaia, H.D. 1962. *Prehistory and Protohistory of India and Pakistan.* Pune.

Schwartz Gazin Amy. (eds). 1999. *Archaeology and Folklore.* Routledge, London.

Seonbok, Y. 2002. Thunder-Axes and the traditional view of Stone tools from Korea. *Journal of East Asian Archeology.* 4 (1-4), pp. 293-306.

Simon, I.M. (ed). 1991. *MEGHALAYA DISTRICT GAZETTERS.* Shilong.

Singh Jai Prakash. (eds). 1991. *Archaeology of North-Eastern India.* New Delhi.

Shadap Sen Cathrine Namita. 1981.*The Origin of the Khais-Synteng People.* Calcutta.

Sharma, A.K. 1996. *Early Man in Eastern Himalayas (North-East India and Nepal).* New Delhi.

Sharma, D.P. 2002. Early Holocene Farming Cultures of North Eastern India. In V.D. Mishra & J.N. Pal (eds) *Mesolithic India.* University of Allahabad, pp 465-484.

Sharma Siddheshwar. 2003. *MEGHALAYA, The Land and Forest (A Remote Sensing Based Study).*Guwahati.

Sharma, T.C. 1967. A Note on Neolithic Pottery of Assam. *Man,* 2(1), pp.126-28.

----1889. Neolithic: eastern region. In A. Gosh (ed) *An Encyclopedia of Indian Archaeology.* 2. New Delhi,pp. 58-60.

----1991. Prehistoric Situation in North-East India. In Jai Prakash Singh & Gautam Sengupta (eds) *Archaeology of North-Eastern India.* New Delhi. pp. 43-52.

Sorenson, P. 1988. *Archaeological Excavation in Thailand.* London.

Steel, E.H. Lt. 1870. Celt found among the Namsang Nagas. *Proceedings of the Asiatic Society of Bengal.* pp. 267-68.

Steward Julian. 1942. The Direct Historical Approach to Archeology. *American Antiquity.* 7, pp. 337-343.

Stiles Daniel. 1977. Ethnoarcheology: A discussion of Methods and Application. *Man.* 12, p.1977.

Syiemlieh David. 1994. The Khasi Iron Culture and Iron Trade with Sylhet in the late 18th Century and early 19th. Century. In (ed), J.B.Bhattacharjee, *Studies in Economic History of North East India.* Shillong

Thomas Julian. 1991. *Understanding the Neolithic.* Routledge, London.

Worman E.C. 1949. The Neolithic problem in the Prehistory of India. *Journal of Washington Academy of Science.* 39, pp. 181-200.

Yule H. 1842. Notes on Iron of the Kasia hills. *Journal of the Asiatic Society of Bengal.* xi, pp. 853-857.

Zvelebil M. 1996. The Agricultural frontier and the transition to farming n the Circum-Baltic region. In D. Harris (ed) *The Origins and the spread of agriculture and pastoralism in Eurasia.* London University pp. 323-325.

Vernacular Literature

Costa, G. 1936. *Ka Riti Jong Ka Ri Ki Laiphew Syiem.* Ka Bynta Kaba Nyngkong. Don Bosco, Shillong.

Lyngdoh Homiwell. 1962. *Ka Niam Khasi.*Shillong.

-----1964. *Ki Syiem Khasi bad Synteng.* Shillong.

Kharakor Philomena. 1988., *Ka Kolshor Khasi kumba paw ha ka Literashor Khasi (1930-1940).* Don Bosco Press, Shillong.

Syiem Jormanik. 1984. *Ka Jingiathuh Khanna pateng shaphang Ki Syiem Ka Hima Mylliem (Naduh 1830-haduh 1960).* Jaiaw Langsning, Shillong.

SOUTH ASIAN ARCHAEOLOGY SERIES

EDITED BY ALOK K. KANUNGO

SAA No 1. Kanungo, Alok Kumar 2004 *Glass Beads in Ancient India: An Ethnoarchaeological Approach* (*British Archaeological Reports, International Series* S1242) Oxford. ISBN 1 84171 364 3.

SAA No 2. Kanungo, Alok Kumar (Ed) 2005 *Gurudakshina: Facets of Indian Archaeology, Essays presented to Prof. V.N. Misra* (*British Archaeological Reports, International Series* S1433) Oxford. ISBN 1 84171 723 1.

SAA No 3. Swayam, S. 2006 *Invisible People: Pastoral life in Proto-Historic Gujurat* (*British Archaeological Reports, International Series* S1464) Oxford. ISBN 1 84171 732 0.

SAA No 4. Mushrif-Tripathy, Veena & Walimbe S.R. 2006 *Human Skeletal Remains from Chalcolithic Nevasa: Osteobiographic Analysis* (*British Archaeological Reports, International Series* S1476) Oxford. ISBN 1 84171 737 1.

SAA No 5. Jahan, Shahnaj Husne 2006 *Excavating Waves and Winds of (Ex)change: A Study of Maritime Trade in Early Bengal* (*British Archaeological Reports, International Series* S1533) Oxford. ISBN 1 84171 753 3.

SAA No 6. Pawankar, Seema J. 2007 *Man and Animal Relationship in Early Farming Communities of Western India, with Special Reference to Inamgaon* (*British Archaeological Reports, International Series* S1639) Oxford. ISBN 978 1 4073 0062 7.

SAA No 7. Sharma, Sukanya 2007 *Celts, Flakes and Bifaces – The Garo Hills Story* (*British Archaeological Reports, International Series* S1664) Oxford. ISBN 978 1 4073 0068 9.

SAA No 8. Kanungo, Alok Kumar (Ed) 2007 *Gurudakshina: Facets of Indian Archaeology, Essays presented to Prof. V.N. Misra* (Part II) (*British Archaeological Reports, International Series* S1665) Oxford. ISBN 978 1 4073 0069 6.

SAA No 9. Nagar, Malti 2008 Hunter-Gatherers in North and Central India: An Ethnoarchaeological Study (*British Archaeological Reports, International Series* S1749) Oxford. ISBN 978 1 4073 0209 6.

SAA No 10. Jahan, Shahnaj Husne (Ed) 2009 Abhijñān: *Studies in South Asian Archaeology and Art History of Artefacts, Felicitating A.K.M. Zakariah.* (*British Archaeological Reports, International Series* S1974) Oxford. ISBN 978 1 4073 0458 8.

SAA No 11. Mitri, Marco 2009 An Outline of the Neolithic Culture of the Khasi-Jaintia Hills of Meghalaya, India: *An Archaeological Investigation.* (*British Archaeological Reports, International Series* S2013) Oxford. ISBN 978 1 4073 0463 2.

www.ingramcontent.com/pod-product-compliance
Lightning Source LLC
Chambersburg PA
CBHW051302270326
41926CB00030B/4691